The Teachings of
Ramana Maharshi

By the same author

Ramana Maharshi and the Path of Self-Knowledge
The Collected Works of Ramana Maharshi
(Edited by Arthur Osborne)

The Teachings of
Ramana Maharshi

Edited by
Arthur Osborne

SAMUEL WEISER, INC.

York Beach, Maine

This edition published in 1996 by
Samuel Weiser, Inc.
P. O. Box 612
York Beach, ME 03910-0612

02 01 00 99 98 97 96
10 9 8 7 6 5 4 3 2 1

Library of Congress Cataloging-in-Publication Data:
Osborne, Arthur
   The teachings of Ramana Maharshi / Arthur Osborne.
      p.   cm.
   Originally published: 1st American ed. 1971.
   Includes index.
      1. Ramana, Maharshi. 2. Spiritual life--Hinduism. I. Title.
BL1175.R342083   1996
294.5'092--dc20   96-14582
                                                            CIP

ISBN 0-87728-897-6
CCP

Printed in the United States of America

The paper used in this publication meets the minimum
requirements of the American National Standard for
Permanence of Paper for Printed Library Materials
Z39.48-1984.

CONTENTS

ABBREVIATIONS

D.D.	*Day by Day with Bhagavan* by Sri A. Devaraja Mudaliar
E.I.*	*Essence of Instruction*
F.H.*	*Five Hymns to Sri Arunachala*
F.V.*	*Forty Verses*
F.V.S.*	*Supplementary Forty Verses*
M.G.	*Maharshi's Gospel*
R.M.	*Ramana Maharshi and the Path of Self-Knowledge* by Arthur Osborne
S.D.B.	*Sad Darsana Bhashya*
S.E.*	*Self-Enquiry*
S.I.	*Spiritual Instruction*
T.	*Talks with Sri Ramana Maharshi*
W.*	*Who am I?*

The titles marked with an asterisk are contained in *The Collected Works of Ramana Maharshi*, originally published by Rider & Co. in England and by Sri Ramanasramam, Tiruvannamalai, in India. (Page numbers refer to the Rider edition.)

The other books are all published by Sri Ramanasramam, except *Ramana Maharshi and the Path of Self-Knowledge* which is presently available from Samuel Weiser. Readers may also find copies of the original Rider edition. (Page numbers refer to both the Weiser and Rider editions.)

PREFACE

During the half-century and more of his life at Tiruvannamalai, Bhagavan Sri Ramana Maharshi was visited by a constant stream of people from all parts of India and by many from the West, seeking spiritual guidance, or consolation in grief, or simply the experience of his presence. He wrote very little all these years, but a number of records of his talks with visitors were kept and subsequently published by his Ashram. These are mostly in diary form, with little arrangement according to subject. The purpose of the present book is to build up a general exposition of the Maharshi's teachings by selecting and fitting together passages from these dialogues and from his writings (published as *The Collected Works of Ramana Maharshi* by Messrs. Rider & Co., in England and by Sri Ramanasramam in India). The editor's comments have been kept to a minimum and are printed in smaller type to distinguish them clearly from the Maharshi's own words.

No distinction is made between the periods at which the Maharshi made any statement, and none is needed, for he was not a philosopher working out a system but a Realized Man speaking from direct knowledge. It sometimes happens that one who is on a spiritual path, or even who has not yet begun consciously seeking, has a glimpse of Realization during which, for a brief eternity, he experiences absolute certainty of his divine, immutable, universal Self. Such an experience came to the Maharshi when he was a lad of seventeen. He himself has described it.

'It was about six weeks before I left Madura for good that the great change in my life took place. It was quite sudden. I was sitting alone in a room on the first floor of my uncle's house. I seldom had any sickness, and on that day there was nothing wrong with my health, but a sudden violent fear of death overtook me. There was nothing in my state of health to account for it, and I did not try to account for it or to find out whether there was any reason for the fear. I just felt "I am going to die" and began thinking what to do about it. It did not occur to me to consult a doctor, or my elders or friends; I felt that I had to solve the problem myself, there and then.

'The shock of the fear of death drove my mind inwards and I said to myself mentally, without actually framing the words: "Now death has come; what does it mean? What is it that is dying? The body dies." And I at once dramatized the occurrence of death. I lay with my limbs stretched out stiff as though *rigor mortis* had set in and imitated a corpse so as to give greater reality to the enquiry. I held my breath and kept my lips tightly closed so that no sound could escape, so that neither the word "I" nor any other word could be uttered. "Well then," I said to myself, "this body is dead. It will be carried stiff to the burning ground and there burnt and reduced to ashes. But with the death of this body am I dead? Is the body I? It is silent and inert but I feel the full force of my personality and even the voice of the 'I' within me, apart from it. So I am Spirit transcending the body. The body dies but the Spirit that transcends it cannot be touched by death. That means I am the deathless Spirit." All this was not dull thought; it flashed through me vividly as living truth which I perceived directly, almost without thought-process. "I" was something very real, the only real thing about my present state, and all the conscious activity connected with my body was centered on that "I". From that moment onwards the "I" or Self focussed attention on itself by a powerful fascination. Fear of death had vanished once and for all. Absorption in the Self continued unbroken from that time on.'[1]

It is the last sentence that is the most remarkable, because usually such an experience soon passes, although the impression

R.M., p. 18

of certainty that it leaves on the mind is never afterwards forgotten. Very rare are the cases when it remains permanent, leaving a man thenceforth in constant identity with the Universal Self. Such a one was the Maharshi.

Soon after this change occurred, the youth who was later to be known as 'the Maharshi' left home as a sadhu. He made his way to Tiruvannamalai, the town at the foot of the holy hill of Arunachala, and remained there for the rest of his life.

For a while he sat immersed in Divine Bliss, not speaking, scarcely eating, utterly neglecting the body he no longer needed. Gradually, however, devotees gathered around him and, for their sake, he returned to an outwardly normal life. Many of them, craving instruction, brought him books to read and expound, and he thus became learned almost by accident, neither seeking nor valuing learning. The ancient teaching of non-duality that he thus acquired merely formalized what he had already realized. He has explained this himself.

'I had read no books except the *Periapuranam*, the Bible and bits of *Tayumanavar* or *Tevaram*. My conception of Ishvara was similar to that found in the Puranas; I had never heard of Brahman, *samsara* and so forth. I did not yet know that there was an Essence or impersonal Real underlying everything and that Ishvara and I were both identical with it. Later, at Tiruvannamalai, as I listened to the *Ribhu Gita* and other sacred books, I learnt all this and found that the books were analysing and naming what I had felt intuitively without analysis or name.'[1]

Perhaps something should be said about the Maharshi's way of answering questions. There was nothing heavy or pontifical about it. He spoke freely and his replies were often given with laughter and humour. If the questioner was not satisfied, he was free to object or ask further questions. It has been said that the Maharshi taught in silence, but this does not mean that he gave no verbal expositions, only that these were not the essential

[1] R.M., p. 23

teaching. That was experienced as a silent influence in the heart. The power of his presence was overwhelming and his beauty indescribable and yet, at the same time, he was utterly simple, utterly natural, unassuming, unpretentious, unaffected.

For the sake of uniformity, the questioner has been referred to in the dialogues in this book as 'D.', standing for devotee, except in cases where the name is given or where for some reason, the word 'devotee' would not apply. The Maharshi has been referred to as 'B.', standing for Bhagavan, since it was usual to address him by this name and in the third person. Actually, it is a word commonly used to mean 'God' but it is used also in those rare cases where a man is felt to be, as Christ put it, 'One with the Father'. It is the same as the name for the Buddha commonly translated into English as the 'Blessed One'.

So far as is possible, Sanskrit words have been avoided, and it usually has been possible. The purpose of this is to make the book easier to read and also to avoid giving the false impression that the quest of Self-Realization is some intricate science which can be understood only with a Sanskrit terminology. It is true that there are spiritual sciences which have a necessary technical terminology, but they are more indirect. The clear and simple truth of non-duality which Bhagavan taught and the direct path of Self-enquiry which he enjoined can be expounded in simple language; and indeed, he himself so expounded them to Western visitors, without having recourse to Sanskrit terminology. In the rare cases where a Sanskrit term has seemed necessary or useful in this book its approximate meaning has been indicated in brackets, so that no glossary is necessary. It may also be remarked that the English words—Enlightenment, Liberation and Self-Realization have all been used with the same meaning, to correspond with the Sanskrit words *Jnana, Moksha* and *Mukti.*

In places where the English of the source quoted seemed infelicitous, it has been altered. This implies no infidelity to the texts since the replies were mostly given in Tamil or other South Indian languages and later rendered into English. The meaning has not been changed.

ARTHUR OSBORNE

I

THE BASIC THEORY

Readers of a philosophical turn of mind may find it strange to see the first chapter of this work entitled 'The Basic Theory'. It may appear to them that the whole work should be devoted to theory. In fact, however, the Maharshi, like every spiritual master, was concerned rather with the practical work of training aspirants than with expounding theory. The theory had importance, but only as a basis for practice.

D.: Buddha is said to have ignored questions about God.

B.: Yes, and because of this he has been called an agnostic. In fact Buddha was concerned with guiding the seeker to realize Bliss here and now rather than with academic discussions about God and so forth.[1]

D.: Is the study of science, psychology, physiology, etc., helpful for attaining yoga-liberation or for intuitive understanding of the unity of Reality?

B.: Very little. Some theoretical knowledge is needed for Yoga and may be found in books, but practical application is what is needed. Personal example and instruction are the most helpful aids. As for intuitive understanding, a person may laboriously convince himself of the truth to be grasped by intuition, of its function and nature, but the actual intuition is more like feeling and requires practice and personal contact. Mere book learning is not of any great use. After Realization all intellectual loads are useless burdens and are to be thrown overboard.[2]

[1] M.G., II, p. 53   [2] T., 28

13

Pre-occupation with theory, doctrine and philosophy can actually be harmful insofar as it detracts a man from the really important work of spiritual effort by offering an easier alternative which is merely mental and which, therefore, cannot change his nature.

'What use is the learning of those who do not seek to wipe out the letters of destiny (from their brow) by enquiring: "Whence is the birth of us who know the letters?" They have sunk to the level of a gramophone. What else are they, O Arunachala?

'It is those who are not learned that are saved rather than those whose ego has not yet subsided in spite of their learning. The unlearned are saved from the relentless grip of the devil of self-infatuation; they are saved from the malady of a myriad whirling thoughts and words; they are saved from running after wealth. It is from more than one evil that they are saved.'[1]

Similarly he had no use for theoretical discussions.

'It is due to illusion born of ignorance that men fail to recognize that which is always and for everybody the inherent Reality dwelling in its natural heart-centre and to abide in it, and that instead they argue that it exists or does not exist, that it has form or has not form, or is non-dual or is dual.[2]

'Can anything appear apart from that which is eternal and perfect? This kind of dispute is endless. Do not engage in it. Instead turn your mind inward and put an end to all this. There is no finality in disputation.'[3]

Ultimately, even the scriptures are useless.

'The scriptures serve to indicate the existence of the Higher Power or Self and to point the way to It. That is their essential purpose. Apart from that they are useless. However, they are voluminous in order to be adapted to the level of development of every seeker. As a man rises in the scale he finds the stages already attained to be only stepping stones to higher stages, until finally the goal is reached. When that happens, the goal alone

[1] F.V.S., 81   [2] F.V., 75   [3] T., 132

remains and everything else, including the scriptures, becomes useless.'[1]

Sometimes, it is true, he expounded philosophy in all its intricacies, but only as a concession to weakness, to those 'addicted to much thinking', as he put it in Self-Enquiry. I had thought of quoting such an explanation here, but found that it contained the passage:

'The intricate maze of philosophy of the various schools is said to clarify matters and to reveal the Truth, but in fact it creates confusion where none need exist. To understand anything there must be the Self. The Self is obvious, so why not remain as the Self? What need to explain the non-self?'

And of himself he adds:

'I was indeed fortunate that I never took to it (i.e. philosophy). Had I taken to it I would probably be nowhere; but my inherent tendencies led me directly to inquire "Who am I?" How fortunate.'[2]

THE WORLD—REAL OR ILLUSION?

Nevertheless, some theoretical teaching is necessary as the basis for the practical work of spiritual training. With the Maharshi this took the form of non-duality, in complete accordance with the teachings of the great Sage, Shankara. The agreement does not, however, mean that Bhagavan was, as a philosopher would put it, 'influenced by' Shankara, merely that he recognized Shankara's teaching as a true exposition of what he had realized and knew by direct knowledge.

D.: Is Bhagavan's teaching the same as Shankara's?
B.: Bhagavan's teaching is an expression of his own experience and realization. Others find that it tallies with Sri Shankara's.[3]

[1] T., 63 [2] T., 392 [3] T., 189

D.: When the Upanishads say that all is Brahman, how can we agree with Shankara that this world is illusory?

B.: Shankara also said that this world is Brahman or the Self. What he objected to is one's imagining that the Self is limited by the names and forms that constitute the world. He only said that the world has no reality apart from Brahman. Brahman or the Self is like a cinema screen and the world like the pictures on it. You can see the picture only so long as there is a screen. But when the observer himself becomes the screen only the Self remains.[1]

'Shankara has been criticized for his philosophy of Maya (illusion) without understanding his meaning. He made three statements: that Brahman is real, that the universe is unreal and that Brahman is the Universe. He did not stop with the second. The third statement explains the first two; it signifies that when the Universe is perceived apart from Brahman, that perception is false and illusory. What it amounts to is that phenomena are real when experienced as the Self and illusory when seen apart from the Self.[2]

'The Self alone exists and is real. The world, the individual and God are, like the illusory appearance of silver in the mother-of-pearl, imaginary creations in the Self.[3] They appear and disappear simultaneously. Actually, the Self alone is the world, the "I" and God. All that exists is only a manifestation of the Supreme.'[4]

D.: What is reality?

B.: Reality must always be real. It has no names or forms but is what underlies them. It underlies all limitations, being itself limitless. It is not bound in any way. It underlies unrealities, being itself Real. It is that which is. It is as it is. It transcends speech and is beyond description such as being or non-being.'[5]

[1] D.D., I, p. 23   [2] R.M., p. 82

[3] As will appear later, this does not in fact imply 'atheism' any more than the previous quotation implies 'pantheism'. In fact, labels are not much use in trying to understand what is not a system of philosophy but a theoretical basis for spiritual effort.

[4] W., p. 42   [5] T., 140

He would not be entangled in apparent disagreements due merely to a different viewpoint or mode of expression.

D.: The Buddhists deny the world whereas Hindu philosophy admits its existence but calls it unreal, isn't that so?

B:. It is only a difference of point of view.

D.: They say that the world is created by Divine Energy (Shakti). Is the knowledge of unreality due to the veiling by illusion (Maya)?

B.: All admit creation by the Divine Energy, but what is the nature of this energy? It must be in conformity with the nature of its creation.

D.: Are there degrees of illusion?

B.: Illusion itself is illusory. It must be seen by somebody outside it, but how can such a seer be subject to it? So, how can he speak of degrees of it?

'You see various scenes passing on a cinema screen; fire seems to burn buildings to ashes; water seems to wreck ships; but the screen on which the pictures are projected remains unburnt and dry. Why? Because the pictures are unreal and the screen real.

'Similarly, reflections pass through a mirror but it is not affected at all by their number or quality.

'In the same way, the world is a phenomenon upon the substratum of the single Reality which is not affected by it in any way. Reality is only One.

'Talk of illusion is due only to the point of view. Change your viewpoint to that of Knowledge and you will perceive the universe to be only Brahman. Being now immersed in the world, you see it as a real world; get beyond it and it will disappear and Reality alone will remain.'[1]

As the last excerpt shows, the postulate of one universal Reality calls for the conception of a process either of illusion or creation to explain the apparent reality of the world.

[1] T., p. 446

'The world is perceived as an apparent objective reality when the mind is externalized, thereby abandoning its identity with the Self. When the world is thus perceived the true nature of the Self is not revealed; conversely, when the Self is realized the world ceases to appear as an objective reality.[1]

'That is illusion which makes one take what is ever present and all pervasive, full to perfection and self-luminous and is indeed the Self and the core of one's Being, for non-existent and unreal. Conversely, that is illusion which makes one take for real and self-existent what is non-existent and unreal, namely the trilogy of world, ego and God.'[2]

The world is indeed real, but not as an independent, self-subsistent reality, just as a man you see in a dream is real as a dream-figure but not as a man.

'To those who have not realized the Self as well as to those who have, the world is real. But to the former, Truth is adapted to the form of the world, whereas to the latter Truth shines as the formless Perfection and the Substratum of the world. This is the only difference between them.'[3]

'As I recalled Bhagavan saying sometimes that unreal (*mithya*, imaginary) and real (*satyam*) mean the same, but did not quite understand, I asked him about it. He said, "Yes, I do sometimes say that. What do you mean by real? What is it that you call real?"

'I answered: "According to Vedanta, only that which is permanent and unchanging can be called real. That is the meaning of Reality."

'Then Bhagavan said: "The names and forms which constitute the world continually change and perish and are therefore called unreal. It is unreal (imaginary) to limit the Self to these names and forms and real to regard all as the Self. The non-dualist says that the world is unreal, but he also says, 'All this is

[1] W., p. 40   [2] S.I., p. 14   [3] F.V., p. 73

Brahman'. So it is clear that what he condemns is regarding the world as objectively real in itself, not regarding it as Brahman. He who sees the Self sees the Self alone in the world also. It is immaterial to the Enlightened whether the world appears or not. In either case, his attention is turned to the Self. It is like the letters and the paper on which they are printed. You are so engrossed in the letters that you forget about the paper, but the Enlightened sees the paper as the substratum whether the letters appear on it or not." '[1]

This is still more succinctly stated as follows :

'The Vedantins do not say that the world is unreal. That is a misunderstanding. If they did, what would be the meaning of the Vedantic text: "All this is Brahman"? They only mean that the world is unreal as the world but real as Self. If you regard world as non-self, it is not real. Everything, whether you call it illusion (*Maya*) or Divine Play (*Lila*) or Energy (*Shakti*) must be within the Self and not apart from it.'[2]

Before leaving the theory of the world as a manifestation of the Self, devoid of objective reality, it must be stressed once again that theory had importance for the Maharshi only insofar as it helped a man's spiritual development, not for its own sake. Cosmology as understood in modern physical science simply did not concern him.

D.: The Vedas contain conflicting accounts of cosmogony. Ether is said to be the first creation in one place, vital energy in another, water in another, something else in another; how can all this be reconciled? Does it not impair the credibility of the Vedas?

B.: Different seers saw different aspects of truth at different times, each emphasizing some viewpoint. Why do you worry about their conflicting statements? The essential aim of the Vedas

[1] D.D., II, p. 264 [2] D.D., I, p. 61

is to teach us the nature of the imperishable Self and show us that we are that.

D.: About that part I am satisfied.

B.: Then treat all the rest as auxiliary arguments or as expositions for the ignorant who want to know the origin of things.[1]

Major Chadwick was copying out the English translation of the Tamil *Kaivalya Navaneetha,* when he came across some of the technical terms in which he found difficulty in understanding. He accordingly asked Bhagavan about them, and Bhagavan replied: 'These portions deal with theories of creation. They are not essential because the real purpose of the scriptures is not to set forth such theories. They mention the theories casually, so that those readers who wish to may take interest in them. The truth is that the world appears as a passing shadow in a flood of light. Light is necessary even to see the shadow. The shadow is not worth any special study, analysis or discussion. The purpose of the book is to deal with the Self and what is said about creation may be omitted for the present.'

Later, Sri Bhagavan continued: 'Vedanta says that the cosmos springs into view simultaneously with him who sees it, and there is no detailed process of creation. It is similar to a dream where he who experiences the dream arises simultaneously with the dream he experiences. However, some people cling so fast to objective knowledge that they are not satisfied when told this. They want to know how sudden creation can be possible and argue that an effect must be preceded by a cause. In fact they desire an explanation of the world that they see about them. Therefore the scriptures try to satisfy their curiosity by such theories. This method of dealing with the subject is called the theory of gradual creation, but the true spiritual seeker can be satisfied with instantaneous creation.'[2]

[1] T., p. 30   [2] T., p. 651.

THE NATURE OF MAN

We come now to the very essence of theory, the nature of man himself. For whatever a man may think of the reality of the world or of God he knows that he himself exists. And it is in order to understand and at the same time to perfect himself that he studies and seeks guidance.

'The individual being which identifies its existence with that of the life in the physical body as "I" is called the ego. The Self, which is pure Consciousness, has no ego-sense about it. Neither can the physical body, which is inert in itself, have this ego-sense. Between the two, that is between the Self or pure Consciousness and the inert physical body, there arises mysteriously the ego-sense or "I" notion, the hybrid which is neither of them, and this flourishes as an individual being. This ego or individual being is at the root of all that is futile and undesirable in life. Therefore it is to be destroyed by any possible means; then That which ever is alone remains resplendent. This is Liberation or Enlightenment or Self-Realization.'[1]

D.: Bhagavan often says: 'The world is not outside you', or 'everything depends on you', or 'what is there outside you'. I find all this puzzling. The world existed before I was born and will continue to exist after my death, as it has survived the death of so many who once lived as I do now.

B.: Did I ever say that the world exists because of you? I have only put to you the question what exists apart from yourself. You ought to understand that by the Self neither the physical body nor the subtle body is meant.

'What you are told is that if you once know the Self within which all ideas exist, not excluding the idea of yourself, of others like you and of the world, you can realize the truth that there is a

[1] S.I., p. 10

Reality, a Supreme Truth, which is the Self of all the world you now see, the Self of all the selves, the one Real, the Supreme, the eternal Self, as distinct from the ego or individual being, which is impermanent. You must not mistake the ego or the bodily idea for the Self.'

D.: Then Bhagavan means that the Self is God?

And in his next reply Bhagavan, as was his way, turned the discussion from theory to practice. Although the present chapter is, on the whole, devoted to theory, it seems appropriate to continue the dialogue so as to show how the theory was put to practical use.

B.: You see the difficulty. Self-enquiry, Who am I? is a different technique from the meditation—'I am Siva', or 'I am He'. I rather emphasize Self-Knowledge, for you are first concerned with yourself before you proceed to know the world or its Lord. The 'I am He' or 'I am Brahman' meditation is more or less mental, but the quest for the Self of which I speak is a direct method and is superior to it. For the moment you get into the quest for the Self and begin to go deeper, the real Self is waiting there to receive you, and then whatever is to be done is done by something else and you, as an individual, have no hand in it. In this process all doubts and discussions are automatically given up, just as one who sleeps forgets all his cares for the time being.

The further discussion illustrates the freedom of argument that Bhagavan allowed to those who were not convinced by a reply.

D.: What certainty is there that something awaits there to receive me?
B.: When a person is sufficiently mature he becomes convinced naturally.
D.: How is this maturity to be attained?
B.: Various ways are prescribed. But whatever previous development there may be, earnest Self-enquiry hastens it.

D.: That is arguing in a circle. I am strong enough for the quest if I am mature and it is the quest that makes me mature.

This is an objection that was often raised in one form or another and the reply to it again emphasizes that it is not theory that is needed but practice.

B.: The mind does have this sort of difficulty. It wants a fixed theory to satisfy itself with. Really, however, no theory is necessary for the man who seriously strives to approach God or his true Self.[1]

'Everyone is the Self and, indeed, is infinite. Yet each person mistakes his body for his Self. In order to know anything, illumination is necessary. This can only be of the nature of Light; however, it lights up both physical light and physical darkness. That is to say, that it lies beyond apparent light and darkness. It is itself neither, but it is said to be light because it illumines both. It is infinite and is Consciousness. Consciousness is the Self of which everyone is aware. No one is ever away from his Self and therefore everyone is in fact Self-realized; only—and this is the great mystery—people do not know this and want to realize the Self. Realization consists only in getting rid of the false idea that one is not realized. It is not anything new to be acquired. It must already exist or it would not be eternal and only what is eternal is worth striving for.

'Once the false notion "I am the body" or "I am not realized" has been removed, Supreme Consciousness or the Self alone remains and in people's present state of knowledge they call this "Realization". But the truth is that Realization is eternal and already exists, here and now.[2]

'Consciousness is pure knowledge. The mind arises out of it and is made up of thoughts.[3]

'The essence of the mind is only awareness or consciousness. However, when the ego overclouds it, it functions as reasoning,

[1] S.D.B. vii, viii   [2] T., p. 482   [3] T., p. 589

thinking or perceiving. The universal mind, not being limited by the ego, has nothing outside itself and is therefore only aware. This is what the Bible means by "I am that I am".

'The ego-ridden mind has its strength sapped and is too weak to resist distressing thoughts. The egoless mind is happy, as we see in deep, dreamless sleep. Clearly, therefore, happiness and distress are only modes of the mind.'[1]

D.: When I seek the 'I' I see nothing.

B.: You say that because you are accustomed to identify yourself with the body and sight with the eyes, but what is there to be seen? And by whom? And how? There is only one Consciousness and this, when it identifies itself with the body, projects itself through the eyes and sees the surrounding objects. The individual is limited to the waking state; he expects to see something different and accepts the authority of his senses. He will not admit that he who sees, the objects seen and the act of seeing are all manifestations of the same Consciousness—the 'I-I'. Meditation helps to overcome the illusion that the Self is something to see. Actually, there is nothing to see. How do you recognize yourself now? Do you have to hold a mirror up in front of yourself to recognize yourself? The awareness is itself the 'I'. Realize it and that is the truth.

D.: When I enquire into the origin of thoughts there is the perception of the 'I' but it does not satisfy me.

B.: Quite right. Because this perception of 'I' is associated with a form, perhaps with the physical body. Nothing should be associated with the pure Self. The Self is the pure Reality in whose light the body, the ego and all else shine. When all thoughts are stilled, pure Consciousness remains over.[2]

D.: How did the ego arise?

Here is a question that gives rise to endless philosophizing, but Bhagavan, holding rigorously to the truth of non-duality, refused to admit its existence.

[1] T., p. 188 [2] T., p. 196

B.: There is no ego. If there were you would have to admit of two selves in you. Therefore there is no ignorance. If you enquire into the Self, ignorance, which is already non-existent, will be found not to exist and you will say that it has fled.

Sometimes it seemed to the listener that absence of thought must mean a mere blank, and therefore Bhagavan specifically guarded against this.

'Absence of thought does not mean a blank. There must be some one to be aware of that blank. Knowledge and ignorance pertain only to the mind and are in duality, but the Self is beyond them both. It is pure Light. There is no need for one Self to see another. There are no two selves. What is not the Self is mere non-self and cannot see the Self. The Self has no sight or hearing; it lies beyond them, all alone, as pure Consciousness.'[1]

Bhagavan often cited man's continued existence during deep, dreamless sleep as a proof that he existed independent of the ego and the body-sense. He also referred to the state of deep sleep as a body-free and ego-free state.

D.: I don't know whether the Self is different from the ego.
B.: In what state were you in deep sleep?
D.: I don't know.
B.: Who doesn't know? The waking self? But you don't deny that you existed while in deep sleep?
D.: I was and am, but I don't know who was in deep sleep.
B.: Exactly. The waking man says that he did not know anything in the state of deep sleep. Now he sees objects and knows that he exists but in deep sleep there were no objects and no spectator. And yet the same person who is speaking now existed in deep sleep also. What is the difference between the two states? There are objects and the play of the senses now, while in deep sleep there were not. A new entity, the ego, has arisen. It acts through the senses, sees objects, confuses itself with the

[1] T., p. 245

body and claims to be the Self. In reality, what was in deep sleep continues to be now also. The Self is changeless. It is the ego which has come between. That which rises and sets is the ego. That which remains changeless is the Self.[1]

Such examples sometimes gave rise to the mistaken idea that the state of Realization or abidance in the Self which Bhagavan prescribed was a state of nescience like physical sleep and therefore he guarded against this also.

B.: Waking, dream and sleep are mere phases of the mind, not of the Self. The Self is the witness of these three states. Your true nature exists in sleep.
D.: But we are advised not to fall asleep during meditation.
B.: It is stupor which you must guard against. That sleep which alternates with waking is not the true sleep. That waking which alternates with sleep is not the true waking. Are you awake now? No. What you have to do is to wake up to your true state. You should neither fall into false sleep nor remain falsely awake.[2]
B.: Though present even in sleep, the Self is not then perceived. It cannot be known in sleep straightaway. It must first be realized in the waking state for it is our true nature underlying all the three states. Effort must be made in the waking state and the Self realized here and now. It will then be understood to be the continuous Self uninterrupted by the alternation of waking, dream and deep sleep.[3]

In fact, one name for the true state of realized being is the Fourth State, existing eternally behind the three states of waking, dream and deep sleep. It is compared with the state of deep sleep, since, like this, it is formless and non-dual; however, as the above quotation shows, it is far from being the same. In the Fourth State the ego merges in Consciousness, as in sleep it does in unconsciousness.

[1] T., p. 143   [2] T., p. 495   [3] T., p. 307

DEATH AND RE-BIRTH

In nothing did Bhagavan show more clearly that theory has to be adapted to the understanding of the seeker than in the question of death and re-birth. For those who were capable of grasping pure, non-dual theory, he explained merely that the question does not arise, for if the ego has no real existence, now, it has none after death either.

D.: Do a person's actions in this life affect him in future births?

B.: Are you born now? Why do you think of future births? The truth is that there is neither birth nor death. Let him who is born think of death and palliatives for it.[1]

D.: Is the Hindu doctrine of reincarnation right?

B.: No definite answer is possible. Even the present incarnation is denied, for instance in the Bhagavad Gita.

D.: Isn't our personality beginningless?

B.: Find out first whether it exists at all and after you have solved that problem, ask the question. Nammalwar says: 'In ignorance, I took the ego to be the Self, but with right knowledge the ego is not and only you remain as the Self.' Both the non-dualists and the dualists agree on the necessity for Self-realization. Attain that first and then raise other questions. Non-dualism or dualism cannot be decided on theoretical grounds alone. If the Self is realized the question will not arise.[2]

'Whatever is born must die; whatever is acquired must be lost; but were you born? You are eternally existent. The Self can never be lost.'[3]

Bhagavan, indeed, discouraged pre-occupation with such questions since they merely distract one from the real task of realizing the Self here and now.

[1] T., p. 17   [2] T., p. 491   [3] T., p. 20

D.: They say that we have the choice of enjoying merit or demerit after our death, that it depends on our choice which comes. Is that so?

B.: Why raise questions of what happens after death? Why ask whether you were born, whether you are reaping the fruits of your past karma, and so on? You will not raise such questions in a little while when you fall asleep. Why? Are you a different person now from the one you are when asleep? No, you are not. Find out why such questions do not occur to you when you are asleep.[1]

On occasion, however, Bhagavan did admit of a lower, contingent point of view for those who could not hold to the doctrine of pure non-dualism.

'In the Bhagavad Gita Sri Krishna first says to Arjuna in Chapter II, that no one was born and then in Chapter IV, "there have been numerous incarnations both of you and me. I know them but you do not." Which of these two statements is true? The teaching varies according to the understanding of the listener.[2]

'When Arjuna said that he would not fight against his relatives and elders in order to kill them and gain the kingdom, Sri Krishna said: "Not that these, you or I, were not before, are not now, nor will be hereafter. None was born, none has died, nor will it be so hereafter." He further developed this theme, saying that he had given instructions to the Sun and through him to Ikshvaku; and Arjuna queried how that could be, since he had been born only a few years back, while they lived ages ago. Then Sri Krishna saw his point of view and said: "Yes, there have been many incarnations of me and you. I know them all but you do not."

'Such statements appear contradictory, but they are true according to the viewpoint of the questioner. Christ also said that he was before Abraham.'[3]

[1] T., p. 242   [2] T., p. 436   [3] T., p. 145

So, from a contingent level, Bhagavan could admit:

'Just as in dreams, you wake up after several new experiences so after death another body is found.[1]

'Just as rivers lose their individuality when they discharge their waters into the ocean, and yet the waters evaporate and return as rain on the hills and back again through the rivers to the ocean, so also individuals lose their individuality when they go to sleep but return again according to their previous innate tendencies. Similarly, in death also, being is not lost.'

D.: How can that be?

B.: See how a tree grows again when its branches are cut off. So long as the life source is not destroyed, it will grow. Similarly, latent potentialities withdraw into the heart at death but do not perish. That is how beings are re-born.[2]

Nevertheless, from the higher viewpoint he would say:

'In truth there is neither seed nor tree, there is only Being.'[3]

He would occasionally explain in more detail, but still with the reservation that in reality there is only the changeless Self.

D.: How long is the interval between death and re-birth?

B.: It may be long or short, but a Realized Man undergoes no such change; he merges into the Infinite Being, as is said in the Brihad Aranyaka Upanishad. Some say that those who, after death, take the path of light are not re-born; whereas those who take the path of darkness are born after they have reaped their karma (self-made destiny) in their subtle bodies.

'If a man's merits and demerits are equal, he is re-born immediately on earth; if the merits outweigh the demerits, his subtle body goes first to heaven, while if the demerits outweigh

[1] T., p. 144   [2] T., p. 108   [3] T., p. 439

the merits he goes first to hell. But in either case he is later re-
born on earth. All this is described in the scriptures, but in fact
there is neither birth nor death; one simply remains what one
really is. That only is the truth.'[1]

Again, he would explain in terms of God's mercy:

B.: God in His mercy withholds this knowledge from people.
If they knew that they had been virtuous they would grow proud,
and in the other case they would be despondent. Both are bad.
It is enough to know the Self.[2]

He did, however, refer sometimes to a person's preparedness or
maturity as being due to the achievements of a previous incarnation.

'A competent person who has already, perhaps in a previous
incarnation, qualified himself realizes the truth and abides in
peace as soon as he hears it told him just once, whereas one who
is not so qualified has to pass through the various stages before
attaining *samadhi* (direct, pure consciousness of being).'[3]

That is to say that a lifetime may be regarded as a day's journey
upon the pilgrimage to Self-realization. How far from the goal one
starts depends on the effort or lack of effort made on the previous days;
how far forward one advances depends on the effort of today.

A Science lecturer from a university asked whether the
intellect survives a man's death and was told:
Why think of death? Consider what happens in your sleep.
What is your experience of that?
D.: But sleep is transient, whereas death is not.
B.: Sleep is intermediate between two waking states, and in
the same way death is intermediate between two births. Both are
transient.
D.: I mean when the spirit is disembodied, does it carry the
intellect with it?

[1]T., p. 573   [2]T., p. 553   [3]T., p. 21

B.: The spirit is not disembodied; the bodies differ. If not a gross body it will be a subtle one, as in sleep, dream or daydream.[1]

Bhagavan would never admit that differences in mode of expression or formulation of doctrine between the various religions signified real contradiction, since the Truth to which they point is One and Immutable.

D.: Is the Buddhist view that there is no continuous entity answering to the idea of the individual soul right or not? Is this consistent with the Hindu doctrine of a reincarnating ego? Is the soul a continuous entity which reincarnates again and again, according to the Hindu doctrine, or is it a mere conglomeration of mental tendencies?

B.: The real Self is continuous and unaffected. The reincarnating ego belongs to a lower plane, that of thought. It is transcended by Self-realization.

'Reincarnations are due to a spurious offshoot of Being and are therefore denied by the Buddhists. The human state is due to a mingling of the sentient with the insentient.'[2]

Sometimes it was not a question of reincarnation but grieving over the death of a loved one. A lady who had come from North India asked Bhagavan whether it was possible to know the posthumous state of an individual.

B.: It is possible, but why try? Such facts are only as real as the person who seeks them.

L.: The birth of a person and his life and death are real to us.

B.: Because you wrongly identify yourself with the body, you think of the other also as a body. Neither you nor he is the body.

[1] T., p. 206 [2] T., p. 136

L.: But from my own level of understanding, I regard myself and my son as real.

B.: The birth of the 'I' thought is a person's birth and its death is his death. After the 'I' thought has arisen, the wrong identification with the body arises. Identifying yourself with the body makes you falsely identify others also with their bodies. Just as your body was born and grows and will die, so you think the other also was born, grew and died. Did you think of your son before he was born? The thought came after his birth and continues even after his death. He is your son only insofar as you think of him. Where has he gone? To the source from which he sprang. So long as you continue to exist, he does too. But if you cease to identify yourself with the body and realize the true Self, this confusion will vanish. You are eternal and others also will be found to be eternal. Until this is realized there will always be grief due to false values which are caused by wrong knowledge and wrong identification.[1]

'On the death of King George V, two devotees were discussing the matter in the hall and seemed upset. Bhagavan said: "What is it to you who dies or is lost? Die yourself and be lost, becoming one with the Self of all (on the ego's extinction)." '[2]

And finally, about the importance of death. Religions stress the importance of the frame of mind in which a person dies and his last thoughts at death. But Bhagavan reminded people that it is necessary to be well prepared beforehand; if not, undesirable tendencies will rise up at death, too powerful to be controlled.

D.: Even if I cannot realize in my lifetime, let me at least not forget on my death-bed. Let me have a glimpse of Reality at least at the moment of death, so that it may stand me in good stead in the future.

B.: It is said in the Bhagavad Gita, Ch. VIII, that whatever is a person's last thought at death determines his next birth. But

[1] T., p. 276   [2] T., p. 236

it is necessary to experience Reality now, in this life, in order to experience it at death. Consider whether this present moment is any different from the last one of death and try to be in the desired state.[1]

HEART AND HEAD

This seems a suitable place to set forth the Maharshi's teaching about heart and head. He taught that the heart, not the head, is the true seat of Consciousness; but by this he did not mean the physical organ at the left side of the chest but the 'spiritual heart' at the right, and by 'consciousness' he did not mean thought but pure awareness or sense of being. He had found this from his own experience to be the centre of spiritual awareness and then found his experience confirmed in some ancient texts. When his devotees were instructed to concentrate on the heart, it was this spiritual heart upon the right that was referred to; and they also would find it the centre of an actual, almost physical vibration of awareness. However, he would also speak of the Heart as equivalent to the Self and remind them that in truth it is not in the body at all but spaceless.

D.: Why do you say that the heart is on the right when biologists have found it to be on the left? What authority have you?

B.: No one denies that the physical organ is on the left; but the heart of which I speak is on the right. That is my experience and I require no authority for it; still, you can find confirmation of it in a Malayali book on Ayurveda and in the Sita Upanishad.[2]

Saying this, Bhagavan showed the quotation from the latter and quoted the text from the former. Sometimes, when asked, he referred also to the Biblical text from Ecclesiastes: 'The wise man's heart is at the right hand and a fool's heart is at the left.'

D.: Why do we have a place such as the heart to concentrate on for meditation?

[1] T., p. 621   [2] T., p. 4

B.: Because you seek true Consciousness. Where can you find it? Can you attain it outside yourself? You have to find it internally. Therefore you are directed inward. The Heart is the seat of Consciousness or Consciousness itself.[1]

'I ask you to observe where the "I" arises in your body, but it is not really quite correct to say that the "I" arises from and merges in the chest at the right side. The Heart is another name for the Reality and this is neither inside nor outside the body. There can be no in or out for it, since it alone is. I do not mean by "heart" any physiological organ or any plexus or nerves or anything like that; but so long as a man identifies himself with the body or thinks he is in the body, he is advised to see where in the body the "I" thought arises and merges again. It must be the heart at the right side of the chest since every man of whatever race and religion and in whatever language he may be speaking, points to the right side of the chest to indicate himself when he says "I". This is so all over the world, so that must be the place. And by keenly watching the emergence of the "I" thought on waking and its subsidence on going to sleep, one can see that it is in the heart on the right side.[2]

'When a room is dark you need a lamp to light it, but when the sun rises there is no need for a lamp; objects are seen without one. And to see the sun itself no lamp is needed because it is self-luminous. Similarly with the mind. The reflected light of the mind is necessary to perceive objects, but to see the heart it is enough for the mind to be turned towards it. Then the mind loses itself and the Heart shines forth.'[3]

It is a yogic practice to concentrate on one of the *chakras* or spiritual centres of the body, very often on the point between the eyebrows. As will be shown in a later chapter, the heart on the right side is not one of these *chakras*; nevertheless, in the following passage, Bhagavan explains concisely his teaching that concentration on the heart-centre

[1] T., p. 205   [2] D.D., I, p. 18   [3] T., p. 99

is more effective than on any other point but less effective than pure enquiry.

D.: There are said to be six (subtle) organs of different colours in the chest, of which the spiritual heart is said to be the one situated two fingers' breadth to the right from the centre. But the heart is also said to be formless. Does that mean that we should imagine it to have a form and meditate on this?

B.: No; only the quest—'Who am I?' is necessary. That which continues to exist throughout sleep and waking is the same being in both; but while waking there is unhappiness and therefore the effort to remove it. When asked who awakes from sleep, you say 'I'. Hold fast to this 'I'. If that is done the Eternal Being reveals itself. The most important thing is the investigation of the 'I' and not concentration on the heart-centre. There is no such thing as the 'inner' and the 'outer'. Both words mean the same or nothing at all. Nevertheless, there is also the practice of concentration on the heart-centre, which is a form of spiritual exercise. Only he who concentrates on the heart can remain aware when the mind ceases to be active and remains still, with no thoughts, whereas those who concentrate on any other centre cannot retain awareness without thought but only infer that the mind was still after it has become active again.[1]

In the following passage an English lady remarks on this awareness without thought and Bhagavan approves.

D.: Thoughts suddenly cease and 'I-I' rises up equally suddenly and continues. It is only a feeling, not a thought. Can it be right?

B.: Yes, it is quite right. Thoughts have to cease and reason to disappear for the 'I-I' to rise up and be felt. Feeling is the main thing, not reason.

D.: Moreover, it is not in the head, but at the right side of the chest.

[1] T., p. 131

B.: That is where it should be, because the heart is there.

D.: When I look outwards it disappears. What should I do?

B.: Hold fast to it.[1]

This does not mean that thought is impossible during the state of 'I' consciousness, as indeed one can see from the example of Bhagavan himself, who was permanently in that state. For the ignorant person, thought is like a dense cloud overhead, shutting him off from the illumination of the sun. When the ceiling of cloud has been broken and rolled back, letting in the light, he can use thought without being imprisoned by it. To change the metaphor, Bhagavan sometimes compared the mind of the Realized Man to the moon in the sky in day-time—it is there but its light is not needed—because one can see without it by the direct light of the sun.

SUFFERING

One of the problems about which Bhagavan was often asked was suffering. The questions were usually personal rather than academic, since it was often the experience of grief which drove people to seek solace from him. The real solace came as a silent influence, but he did also answer theoretical questions. The usual answer was to bid the questioner find out who it is that suffers, just as he would bid the doubter find who it is that doubts; for the Self is beyond suffering as it is beyond doubt. Sometimes, however, on a more contingent level, he would point out that whatever makes a person dissatisfied with his state of ignorance and turns him to the quest of the Self is beneficial and that it is often suffering which is the means of doing this.

B.: The Bliss of Self is always yours and you will find it if you seek it earnestly. The cause of your misery is not in your outer life; it is in you, as your ego. You impose limitations on yourself and then make a vain struggle to transcend them. All unhappiness is due to the ego. With it comes all your trouble.

[1] T., p. 24

What does it avail you to attribute the cause of misery to the happenings of life when that cause is really within you? What happiness can you get from things extraneous to yourself? When you get it how long will it last?

'If you would deny the ego and scorch it by ignoring it you would be free. If you accept it, it will impose limitations on you and throw you into a vain struggle to transcend them. That was how the "thief" sought to ruin King Janaka.

'To be the Self that you really are is the only means to realize the Bliss that is ever yours.'[1]

'A very devoted and simple devotee had lost his only son, a child of three. The next day he arrived at the Asramam with his family. Referring to them, Bhagavan said: "Training of mind helps one to bear sorrows and bereavements with courage; but the loss of one's children is said to be the worst of all griefs. Grief only exists as long as one considers oneself to have a definite form; if the form is transcended, one knows the One Self to be eternal. There is neither death nor birth. What is born is only the body and this is the creation of the ego. But the ego is not ordinarily perceived without the body and so is identified with it. It is thought that matters. Let the sensible man consider whether he knew his body while in deep sleep. Why, then, does he feel it in the waking state? Although the body was not felt in sleep, did not the Self exist? What was his state when in deep sleep and what is it now when awake? What is the difference? The ego rises up and that is waking. Simultaneously thoughts arise. Find out who has the thoughts. Where do they come from? They must arise from the conscious self. Apprehending this even vaguely helps towards the extinction of the ego. The realization of the One Infinite Existence becomes possible. In that state there are no individuals but only Eternal Being. Hence there is no thought of death or grieving.

'If a man thinks that he is born he cannot escape the fear of

[1] M.G., II, p. 49

death. Let him find out whether he was ever born or whether the Self takes birth. He will discover that the Self always exists and that the body which is born resolves itself into thought, and that the emergence of thought is the root of all mischief. Find where thought comes from, and then you will abide in the ever-present inmost Self and be free from the idea of birth and fear of death.'[1]

D.: If some one we love dies, it causes grief. Should we avoid such grief by either loving all alike or not loving at all?

B.: If someone we love dies, it causes grief to the one who continues living. The way to get rid of grief is not to continue living. Kill the griever, and who will then remain to grieve? The ego must die. That is the only way. The two alternatives you suggest amount to the same. When all are realized to be the one Self, who is there to love or hate?[2]

Sometimes, however, the questions were informal, referring not to some private tragedy but to the evil and suffering in the world. In such cases they were usually by visitors who did not understand the doctrine of non-duality or follow the path of Self-enquiry.

Visitor: Widespread distress, such as famine and pestilence, spreads havoc through the world. What is the cause of this state of affairs?

B.: To whom does all this appear?

V.: That won't do. I see misery all round.

B.: You were not conscious of the world and its sufferings while asleep, but you are now that you are awake. Continue in the state in which you are not affected by such things. When you are not aware of the world, that is to say when you remain as the Self in the state of sleep, its sufferings do not affect you. Therefore turn inwards and seek the Self and there will be an end both of the world and of its miseries.

V.: But that is selfishness.

[1] T., p. 80   [2] T., p. 252

B.: The world is not external to you. Because you wrongly identify yourself with the body, you see the world outside you and its suffering becomes apparent to you; but the world and its sufferings are not real. Seek the reality and get rid of this unreal feeling.

This the visitor was unwilling to do, but instead referred again to suffering and to those who strive vainly to remove it.

V.: There are great men and public workers who cannot solve the problem of suffering in the world.

B.: That is because they are based on the ego. If they remained in the Self it would be different.

Still presuming the absolute reality of the objective world, the visitor now asked in an indirect way how it would be different, demanding that those who abide in the Self should accept the unreal as Real.

V.: Why don't Mahatmas help?

For the moment, Bhagavan answers on the visitor's own level.

B.: How do you know that they don't? Public speeches, outer activity and material help are all outweighed by the silence of the Mahatmas. They accomplish more than others.

Now, the visitor comes to the practical point: outer activity instead of inner quest; and Bhagavan rejects that viewpoint no less categorically.

V.: What can we do to ameliorate the condition of the world?

B.: If you remain free from pain there will be no pain anywhere. The trouble now is due to your seeing the world outside yourself and thinking there is pain in it. But both the world and the pain are within you. If you turn inwards there will be no pain.

V.: God is perfect. Why did he create the world imperfect?

A work partakes of the nature of its author, but in this case it is not so.

B.: Are you something separate from God that you should ask this question? So long as you consider yourself the body, you see the world as external to you. It is to you that the imperfection appears. God is perfection and his work is also perfection but you see it as imperfect because of your wrong identification with the body or the ego.

V.: Why did the Self manifest as this miserable world?

B.: In order that you might seek it. Your eyes cannot see themselves but if you hold a mirror in front of them they see themselves. Creation is the mirror. See yourself first and then see the whole world as the Self.

V.: Then what it amounts to is that I should always turn inwards?'

B.: Yes.

V.: Shouldn't I see the world at all?

B.: You are not told to shut your eyes to the world, but only to see your Self first and then see the whole world as the Self. If you consider yourself as the body the world appears to be external; if you are the Self the world appears as Brahman manifested.[1]

The trouble is that it is extremely difficult to regard the body or the objective world as unreal. Bhagavan admitted that in the following dialogue.

D.: I have a toothache; is that only a thought?

B.: Yes.

D.: Then why can't I think that there is no toothache, and so cure myself?

B.: One does not feel the toothache when one is absorbed in other thoughts or when asleep.

D.: But still it remains.

B.: So strong is man's conviction of the reality of the world

[1] T., p. 272

that it is not easily shaken off. But the world is no more real than the individual who sees it.

Then a humorous exchange which illustrates the difficulty of the concept.

D.: At present there is a Sino-Japanese war going on. If it is only in the imagination, can or will Sri Bhagavan imagine it not to be going on and so put an end to it?

B. (laughing): The Bhagavan of the questioner (whom the questioner sees as an external being) is as much a thought of his as the Sino-Japanese War![1]

Finally a quotation which shows how Bhagavan sometimes answered on a more contingent plane, pointing out that it is suffering that makes a man discontented with the life of the ego and spurs him on to seek Self-realization.

D.: But why should there be suffering now?

B.: If there were no suffering, how could the desire to be happy arise? If that desire did not arise, how could the quest of the Self arise?

D.: Then is all suffering good?

B.: Yes. What is happiness? Is it a healthy and handsome body, regular meals and so on? Even an emperor has endless troubles, although he may be in good health. So all suffering is due to the false notion 'I am the body'. Getting rid of this is knowledge.[2]

SIN

Sin and evil of every kind are the result of egoism unrestrained by consideration for the injury caused to others or the deleterious effect on the sinner's own character. Religions guard against them by moral and disciplinary codes and emotional appeals, seeking to keep the ego

[1] T., p. 451   [2] T., p. 633

within bounds and prevent its trespassing into forbidden places. However, a spiritual path that is so radical and direct as to deny the ego
itself does not need to attend specifically to the various excesses of
egoism. All egoism has to be renounced. Therefore non-duality turns
the attack on the ego itself, not on its specific manifestations.

'However sinful a person may be, if he would stop wailing
inconsolably: "Alas, I am a sinner; how shall I attain liberation?"
and, casting away even the thought that he is a sinner, if he would
zealously carry on meditation on the Self, he would most assuredly
get reformed.'[1]

Similarly, a discipline which aims at transcending thought completely, in realization of the super-rational Self, does not need to in-
veigh specifically against evil thoughts. All thoughts are distractions.
A European lady asked whether good thoughts were not helpful in
seeking Realization, at any rate in the early stages, like the lower
rungs of the ladder, and was told:

'Yes, insofar as they keep off bad thoughts; but they themselves must disappear before the state of Realization.[2]
'Because the quality of purity (sattva) is the real nature of
the mind clearness like that of the unclouded sky is the characteristic of the mind-expanse. Being stirred up by the quality of
activity (rajas) the mind becomes restless and, influenced by
darkness (tamas), manifests as the physical world. The mind
thus becoming restless on the one hand and appearing as solid
matter on the other, the Real is not discerned. Just as fine silk
threads cannot be woven with the use of a heavy iron shuttle, or
the delicate shades of a work of art be distinguished in the light
of a lamp flickering in the wind, so is Realization of Truth impossible with the mind rendered gross by darkness (tamas) and
restless by activity (rajas). Because truth is exceedingly subtle
and serene, Mind will be cleared of its impurities only by a
desireless performance of duties during several births, getting a
worthy Master, learning from him and incessantly practising

[1] W., p. 44   [2] T., p. 341

meditation on the Supreme. The transformation of the mind into the world of inert matter due to the quality of darkness (*tamas*) and its restlessness due to the quality of activity (*rajas*) will cease. Then the mind regains its subtlety and composure. The Bliss of the Self can manifest only in a mind rendered subtle and steady by assiduous meditation. He who experiences that Bliss is liberated even while still alive.'[1]

He did, of course, insist on the need for purity. Sometimes a visitor would complain that he was too weak to resist his lower tendencies and would simply be told to try harder. According to his temperament he might be told to find who it is that has the lower tendencies, or to trust in God.

D.: I am a sinner and do not perform any religious duties. Shall I have a painful rebirth because of that?

B.: Why do you say you are a sinner? Faith in God is enough to save you from rebirth. Cast all your burden on Him. In the *Tiruvachakam* it is said: 'Though I am worse than a dog, You have graciously undertaken to protect me. The delusion of death and birth is maintained by You. Is it for me to sit and judge? Am I the Lord here? Almighty God, it is for You to roll me through many bodies, or keep me fixed at Your feet.' Therefore have faith and that will save you.[2]

D.: There is more pleasure in meditation than in sensual enjoyment and yet the mind seeks the latter and not the former. Why is that?

B.: Pleasure and pain are only aspects of the mind. Our essential nature is happiness, but we have forgotten the Self and imagine that the body or the mind is the Self. It is this wrong identification that gives rise to misery. What is to be done? This tendency is very deep-rooted and has continued for many past births and so has grown strong. It will have to go before the essential nature, which is happiness, can be realized.[3]

And above all, not to create new *vasanas* or latent tendencies.

[1] S.E., p. 32   [2] T., p. 30   [3] T., p. 540

D.: Swami, how can the grip of the ego be loosened?

B.: By not adding new *vasanas* to it.[1]

If the objective reality of the world be an illusion then the evil in it is also an illusion and the remedy is to turn inwards to the Reality of the Self. An American visitor, the secretary of Swami Yogananda, asked why there are good and evil in the world and was told:

'They are relative terms. There must be a subject to know the good and evil. That subject is the ego. It ends in the Self. Or, you can say that the source of the ego is God. This definition is probably more definite and understandable for you.'[2]

GOD

Superficially, it might seem that the Maharshi's statements about God were inconsistent, since he would sometimes enjoin complete faith and submission to God and sometimes speak of God as unreal; but actually there was no inconsistency. It must always be remembered that the purpose of his exposition was not to propound a philosophy but to give practical guidance on the spiritual path. Someone who could conceive of the non-dual Self could understand that it was his own Self and the Self of God and of the world also, whereas one who clung to the apparent reality of his ego could understand the Self only as the God who had created him. According to their needs he explained. In this, as in other matters, he pointed out the uselessnes of discussion. Following either path was useful; theorizing about them was not.

'All religions postulate the three fundamentals, the world, the soul and God; but it is the One Reality that manifests itself as these three. One can say: "The three are really three" only so long as the ego lasts. Therefore to inhere in one's own Being, when the ego is dead is the perfect state.

'The world is real,' 'No, it is mere illusory appearance,' 'The

[1] T., p. 173   [2] T., p. 106

world is conscious,' 'No,' 'The world is happiness,' 'No,'—What use is it to argue thus? That state is agreeable to all wherein, having given up the objective outlook, one knows one's Self and loses all notions either of unity or duality, of oneself and the ego.

'If one has form oneself, the world and God will also appear to have form; but if one is formless, who is to see these forms, and how? Without the eye can any object be seen? The seeing Self is the Eye, and that Eye is the Eye of Infinity.[1]

'Brahman is not to be seen or known. It is beyond the three-fold relationship of seer, sight and seen, or knower, knowledge and known. The Reality remains ever as it is. The existence of ignorance or the world is due to our illusion. Neither knowledge nor ignorance is real; what lies beyond them, as beyond all other pairs of opposites, is the Reality. It is neither light nor darkness but beyond both, though we sometimes speak of it as light and of ignorance as its shadow.'[2]

When there was genuine search for understanding, Bhagavan would explain in some detail, always leading the seeker back to the doctrine of the One Self.

'Mr. Thompson, a very quiet young gentleman who has been staying in India for some years and studying Hindu philosophy as an earnest student, asked: Srimad Bhagavad Gita says: "I am the prop for Brahman." In another place it says: "I am in the heart of each one." Thus the different aspects of the Ultimate Principle are revealed. I take it that there are three aspects, namely: (1) the transcendental, (2) the immanent, and (3) the cosmic. Is Realization to be in any of these or in all of them? Coming to the transcendental from the cosmic, Vedanta discards the names and forms as being *maya*. Again Vedanta also says that the whole is Brahman, as illustrated by gold and ornaments of gold. How are we to understand the truth'

[1] F.V., p. 72 [2] D.D., I, p. 38

B.: The Gita says: *Brahmano hi pratishtaham.* If that *aham* is known, the whole is known.

D.: That is the immanent aspect only.

B.: You now think that you are an individual; outside you there is the universe and beyond the universe is God. So, there is the idea of separateness. This idea must go. For God is not separate from you or the cosmos. The Gita also says:

'I am the Self, O Gudakesa, seated in the heart of all beings: I am the beginning and the middle and also the end of all beings.[1]

Thus God is not only in the heart of all, He is the prop of all, He is the source of all, their abiding place and their end. All proceed from Him, have their stay in Him, and finally resolve into Him. Therefore He is not separate.

D.: How are we to understand the line in the *Gita:* 'This whole cosmos forms a particle of me'?

B.: It does not mean that a small particle of God separates Him and forms the universe. His shakti is acting; and as a result of one phase of such activity the cosmos has become manifest. Similarly the statement in *Purusha Sukta: Padosya viswa bhutani* (All beings form one of His feet) does not mean that Brahman is in four parts.

D.: I understand that. Brahman is certainly not divisible.

B.: So the fact is that Brahman is all and remains indivisible. He is ever realized. However, man does not know this; and it is just what he has to know. Knowledge means overcoming the obstacles which obstruct the revelation of the Eternal Truth that Self is the same as Brahman. The obstacles taken altogether form your idea of separateness as an individual. Therefore the present attempt will result in the truth being revealed that the Self is not separate from Brahman.[2]

Christians, except for the greatest mystics, cling to the idea of a permanently real and separate ego. Sri Bhagavan had a discussion on this point with a Jesuit Father, but it remained inconclusive, Bhagavan trying to turn the father's mind inwards to Self-inquiry and the father demanding a theoretical exposition instead.

[1] B.G., X., p. 20   [2] T., p. 649

'Dr. Emile Gathier, s.j., Professor of Philosophy at the Sacred Heart College, Shembaganur, Kodaikanal, asked: Can you kindly give me a summary of your teachings?'

B.: They are found in the booklets, particularly in 'Who am I?'

F.: I shall read them. But may I have the central point of your teachings from your own lips?

B.: The central point is just the thing.

F.: It is not clear to me what you mean by that.

B.: That you should find the centre.

F.: I come from God. Isn't God distinct from me?

B.: Who asks this question? God does not. You do. So find who you are and then you may find out whether God is distinct from you.

F.: But God is perfect and I am imperfect. How can I ever know Him fully?

B.: God does not say so. It is you who ask the question. After finding out who you are, you may know what God is.

F.: But you have found your Self. Please let us know if God is distinct from you.

B.: It is a matter of experience. Each one must experience it for himself.

F.: Oh! I see. God is infinite and I am finite. I have a personality which can never merge into God. Isn't that so?

B.: Infinity and perfection do not admit of parts. If a finite being is apart from Infinity, the perfection of Infinity is marred. Thus your statement is a contradiction in terms.

F.: No, see, there is both God and creation.

B.: How are you aware of your personality?

F.: I have a soul. I know it by its activities.

B.: Did you know it in deep sleep?

F.: The activities are suspended in deep sleep.

B.: But you exist in sleep, and you do now too. Which of these two is your real state?

F.: Sleep and waking are mere accidents. I am the substance behind the accidents.

(He looked up at the clock and said that it was time for him to catch the train. He left after thanking Sri Bhagavan. So the conversation ended abruptly.)[1]

The following talk takes up various problems which plague philosophers and theologians—Divine Omniscience and free-will; natural laws and divine activity; personal God and impersonal; and yet the tone of the answer shows that Bhagavan considers it of rather secondary importance.

D.: What is the relation between my free-will and the over-shadowing might of the Omnipotent? (a) Is the Omnipotence of God consistent with the ego's free-will? (b) Is the Omniscience of God consistent with the ego's free-will? (c) Are natural laws consistent with God's free-will?

B.: Yes. Free-will is the present appearing to a limited faculty of sight and will. That same ego sees its past activity as falling into a course of "law" or rules—its own free-will being one of the links in the course of law. The Omnipotence and Omniscience of God are then seen by the ego to have acted through the appearance of his own free-will. So he comes to the conclusion that the ego must go by appearances. Natural laws are manifestations of God's will and they have been laid down.[2]

The following dialogue is characteristic as showing refusal to discuss theory and insistence on the need for practice.

D.: Is God personal?

B.: Yes, He is always the first person, the I, ever standing before you. Because you give precedence to worldly things, God appears to have receded to the background. If you give up all else and seek Him alone, He will remain as the 'I', the Self.

D.: The final state of Realization is said, according to Advaita,

[1] T., p. 602 [2] T., p. 28

to be absolute union with the Divine, and according to Visish-
tadvaita a qualified union, while Dvaita maintains that there is
no union at all. Which of these should be considered the correct
view?

B.: Why speculate about what will happen some time in
the future? All are agreed that the 'I' exists. To whichever school
of thought he may belong, let the earnest seeker first find out what
the 'I' is. Then it will be time enough to know what the final
state will be, whether the 'I' will get merged in the Supreme
Being or stand apart from Him. Let us not forestall the conclusion, but keep an open mind.

D.: But will not some understanding of the final state be a
helpful guide even to the aspirant?

B.: No purpose is served by trying to decide now what the
final state of Realization will be. It has no intrinsic value.

D.: Why not?

B.: Because you proceed on a wrong principle. Your conclusion is arrived at by the intellect which shines only by the
light it derives from the Self. Is it not presumptuous on the part
of the intellect to sit in judgement over that from which it derives
its little light? How can the intellect, which can never reach the
Self, be competent to ascertain and much less decide the nature
of the final state of Realization? It is like trying to measure the
sunlight at its source by the standard of the light given by a candle.
The wax will melt down before the candle comes anywhere near
the sun. Instead of indulging in mere speculation, devote yourself here and now to the search for the Truth that is ever within
you.[1]

Sometimes questions were also asked about the multiple gods of
Hinduism. In this connection it should be explained that Hindus, like
Christians or Muslims, worship the One God. Some of the questions
about God recorded above were put by Hindus. However, they also
worship God manifested in various forms, one possibility or name or
form or viewpoint not negating another.

[1] M.G., II, p. 60

D.: Why are so many gods mentioned?

B.: The body is only one, but how many functions are performed by it! The source of all these functions is one. It is the same with the gods.[1]

It would sometimes be asked whether the various gods and their heavens were real. But such a question starts from the presumption of the reality of this physical world and the questioner's body—a presumption which Bhagavan would not admit. Instead, he would turn this question like all others, to the quest for Reality.

D.: Are the Gods, Ishvara and Vishnu, and their heavens, Kailas and Vaikuntha, real?

B.: As real as you are in this body.

D.: I mean have they got a phenomenal existence like my body, or are they pure fictions like the horns of a hare?

B.: They do exist.

D.: If so they must be somewhere; where are they?

B.: In you.

D.: Then they are only my idea; something which I create and control?

B.: Everything is.

D.: But I can create a pure fiction, like the horns of a hare, or a partial truth, like a mirage; while there are also facts which exist irrespective of my imagination. Do the gods, Ishvara and Vishnu, exist like that?

B.: Yes.

D.: Is God subject to cosmic dissolution at the end of a cycle?

B.: Why should He be? A man who realizes the Self transcends cosmic dissolution and is liberated; why should not Ishvara (God) who is infinitely wiser and abler than a man?

D.: Do gods and devils also exist?

B.: Yes.

[1] T., p. 371

D.: How are we to conceive of Supreme Divine Consciousness?

B.: As that which is.[1]

Particularly interesting are the questions asked by a Muslim professor about the hymns which Bhagavan wrote to God in the form of Arunachala.

D.: I have been reading the Five Hymns. I find that the hymns are addressed by you to Arunachala. But you are a non-dualist, so how can you address God as a separate Being?

B.: The devotee, God and the hymns are all the Self.

D.: But you are addressing God. You are specifying this Arunachala Hill as God.

B.: You can identify the Self with the body, so why shouldn't the devotee identify the Self with Arunachala?

D.: If Arunachala is the Self, why should it be specifically picked out among so many other hills? God is everywhere. Why do you specify Him as Arunachala?

B.: What has attracted you from Allahabad to this place? What has attracted all these people around?

D.: Sri Bhagavan.

B.: How was I attracted here? By Arunachala. The Power cannot be denied. Again Arunachala is within and not without. The Self is Arunachala.

D.: Several terms are used in the holy books, *Atman, Paramatman, Para,* etc. What is the gradation among them?

B.: They mean the same to the user of the words, but they are understood differently by various persons according to their development.

D.: But why do you use so many words to mean the same thing?

B.: It depends on the circumstances. They all mean the Self. *Para* means not relative, or beyond the relative, that is to say the Absolute.[2]

[1] T., p. 30   [2] T., p. 273

Bhagavan would often make remarks, which the superficial critic might take to be agnostic or theistic, just as has been done by superficial critics of the Buddha. For instance he might say:

'Why worry about God? We do not know whether God exists but we know that we exist, so first concentrate on yourself. Find out who you are.'

There was no agnosticism, since Bhagavan, like the Buddha, spoke from perfect knowledge. He was simply placing himself in the position of the questioner and advising him to concentrate rather on what he knew than what he merely believed in. Sometimes he would tell people not to trouble whether there is God or not or whether Realization implies unity with God or not but simply strive to realize the Self, and when that was achieved they would know. Theorizing about it would not help them.

'The Malayalam version of *Ulladu Narpadu* (Forty Verses) was read out by a devotee for the benefit of a visitor. After hearing it, the latter asked: What about the reference to duality during one's effort and unity at the end?'

B.: It refers to people who think one must begin one's spiritual striving with a dualistic idea. They say that there is God and that one must worship and meditate until ultimately the individual merges into God. Others say that the individual and the Supreme Being always remain separate and never merge. But let's not worry now about what happens at the end. All agree that the individual exists now. So let a man discover it—that is discover his Self. There will be time enough afterwards to find out whether the Self is to merge in the Supreme or is a part of it or remains separate. Let us not forestall the conclusion. Keep an open mind, dive within and find the Self. The truth will dawn upon you all right, so why try to decide beforehand whether it is absolute or qualified unity or duality? There is no meaning in doing so. Your decision would have to be made by logic and intellect, but the intellect derives its light from the Self (the Highest Power), so how can its reflected and partial light envisage the entire and original light? The intellect cannot attain to the Self, so how can it ascertain its nature?[1]

While explaining to an American lady, Bhagavan said:

'The Self alone is Real. All else is unreal. The mind and intellect have no existence apart from you. The Bible says: "Be still and know that I am God." Stillness is the only thing needed to realize that I am is GOD.'

Later he added:

'The whole Vedanta is contained in the two Biblical statements "I am that I am" and "Be still and know that I am God".'[2]

For one who found Self-enquiry too difficult, he would recommend worship and submission.

D.: What should one think of when meditating?
B.: What is meditation? It is the suspension of thoughts. You are perturbed by thoughts which rush one after another. Hold on to one thought so that others are expelled. Continuous practice gives the necessary strength of mind to engage in meditation. Meditation differs according to the degree of advancement of the seeker. If one is fit for it one can hold directly to the thinker; and the thinker will automatically sink into his source, which is Pure Consciousness. If one cannot directly hold on to the thinker, one must meditate on God; and in due course the same individual will have become sufficiently pure to hold to the thinker and sink into the absolute Being.[3]

In case the path of worship was chosen, he demanded absolute surrender.

[1] T., p. 63   [2] T., p. 338   [3] T., p. 453

D.: God is described as manifest and unmanifest. As the former, He is said to include the world as a part of His Being. If that is so, we, as part of the world, should find it easy to know Him in His manifested form.

B.: Know yourself before you seek to know the nature of God and the world.

D.: Does knowing myself imply knowing God?

B.: Yes, God is within you.

D.: Then, what stands in the way of my knowing myself or God?

B.: Your wandering mind and perverted ways.

D.: I am a weak creature. But why does not the superior power of the Lord within remove the obstacles?

B.: Yes, He will, if you have the aspiration.

D.: Why should He not create the aspiration in me?

B.: Then surrender yourself.

D.: If I surrender myself, is no prayer to God necessary?

B.: Surrender itself is a mighty prayer.

D.: But is it not necessary to understand His nature before one surrenders oneself?

B.: If you believe that God will do all the things that you want Him to do, then surrender yourself to Him. Otherwise let God alone, and know yourself.[1]

If there be true surrender, there can be no complaint or frustration.

D.: We are worldly people and are afflicted by some grief that we cannot get over. We pray to God and are still not satisfied. What should we do?

B.: Trust God.

D.: We surrender but still there is no help.

B.: But if you have surrendered it means that you must accept the will of God and not make a grievance of what may not happen to please you. Things may turn out differently

[1] M.G., p. 53

from what they appear. Distress often leads people to faith in God.

D.: But we are worldly people. We have wife, children, friends and relations. We cannot ignore them and resign ourselves to the Divine Will without retaining some trace of individuality.

B.: That means that you have not really surrendered, as you say you have. All you need to do is to trust God.[1]

Following the path of devotion, one should leave everything to God.

'The Lord bears the burden of the world. Know that the spurious ego which presumes to bear that burden is like a sculptured figure at the foot of a temple tower which appears to sustain the tower's weight. Whose fault is it if the traveller instead of putting his luggage in the cart which bears the load any way, carries it on his head, to his own inconvenience?'[2]

There cannot even be impatience for speedy realization. To one who was so afflicted, he replied:

'Surrender to Him and accept His will whether He appears or vanishes. Await His pleasure. If you want him to do as you want, it is not surrender but command. You cannot ask Him to obey you and yet think you have surrendered. He knows what is best and when and how to do it. Leave everything entirely to Him. The burden is His and you have no more cares. All your cares are His. That is what is meant by surrender.'[3]

Even prayer can betoken a lack of trust and Bhagavan did not normally encourage prayer in the sense of petition.

'They pray to God and finish with: "Thy will be done." If His will be done why do they pray at all? It is true that the

[1] T., p. 43   [2] F.V.S., p. 79   [3] T., p. 450

Divine will prevails at all times and under all circumstances. Individuals cannot act of their own accord. Recognize the force of the Divine will and keep quiet. Everyone is looked after by God. He created all. You are only one among two thousand millions. When He looks after so many, will He omit you? Even common sense dictates that one should accept His will.

'There is no need to tell Him your requirements. He knows them Himself and will look after them.'[1]

On other occasions, however, he would confirm the efficacy of prayer. As in other matters, he would put the viewpoint which would best help the spiritual development of the particular questioner.

D.: Are your prayers granted?
B.: Yes, they are granted. No thought will ever go in vain. Every thought will produce its effect some time or other. Thought force will never go in vain.[2]

It will be seen that this hints at a doctrine far wider than personal response by an anthropomorphic God. It indicates the general power of thought for good or evil and its repercussions on the thinker. Understanding of this involves a great responsibility for thoughts no less than for actions, just as Christ indicated that to look at a woman lustfully was a sin, the same as committing adultery with her. The following passage shows how far this teaching was from any humanized conception of a God.

'Not from any desire, resolve, or effort on the part of the rising sun, but merely due to the presence of his rays, the lens emits heat, the lotus blossoms, water evaporates and people attend to their various duties in life. In the proximity of the magnet the needle moves. Similarly, the soul or *jiva* subjected to the threefold activity of creation, preservation and destruction which takes place merely due to the unique Presence of the Supreme Lord, performs acts in accordance with its karma, and

[1] T., p. 594   [2] D.D., I, p. 58

subsides to rest after such activity. But the Lord Himself has no resolve; no act or event touches even the fringe of His Being. This state of immaculate aloofness can be likened to that of the sun, which is untouched by the activities of life, or to that of the all-pervasive ether, which is not affected by the interaction of the complex qualities of the other four elements.'[1]

RELIGIONS

It should be clear from what was said in the previous section that Bhagavan's teaching was not opposed to any religion. If philosophers or theologians wished to argue whether the human soul was permanently and essentially separate from the Divine Being, he would refuse to join issue with them but try to turn them to spiritual effort instead, as, for instance, in his talk with a Catholic priest on page 47. When they attained Realization they would know, and theoretical knowledge without Realization would not help them anyway.

Strictly speaking, Bhagavan was not exclusively a Hindu or subject to Hindu ritual, since Hinduism recognizes that one who is established in constant, conscious identity with the Self is above all religions; he is the mountain peak towards which the various paths converge. Bhagavan had many followers who were not Hindus—Christians, Muslims, Parsis and others—and none was ever recommended to change his religion.

A religion involves two modes of activity; what might be called the horizontal and the vertical. Horizontally it harmonizes and controls the life of the individual and society in conformity with its faith and morality, giving opportunity and incentive for a good life leading to a good death. Vertically it provides spiritual paths for those who strive to attain a higher state or realize the ultimate truth during this life on earth. Horizontally, religions are mutually exclusive, but not really contradictory. Bhagavan was concerned rather with the vertical mode, the paths to realization, and therefore his teaching clashed with no religion. He guided those who would follow him on

[1] W., p. 46

the most direct and central path, the quest of the Self; and for this any religion could serve as a foundation. He approved of every religion and if some devotees came to him who followed no formal religion, he did not insist they should do so. When asked about the different religious practices, he would stress their deeper meaning, and about different religions their basic unity.

D.: What is yoga?

B.: Yoga (union) is necessary for one who is in a state of *viyoga* (separation). But really there is only One. If you realize the Self there will be no difference.

D.: Is there any efficacy in bathing in the Ganges?

B.: The Ganges is within you. Bathe in this Ganges; it will not make you shiver with cold.

D.: Should we sometimes read the Bhagavad Gita?

B.: Always.

D.: May we read the Bible?

B.: The Bible and the Gita are the same.

D.: The Bible teaches that man is born in sin.

B.: Man is sin. There is no feeling of being man in deep sleep. The body-thought brings out the idea of sin. The birth of thought itself is sin.

D.: The Bible says that the human soul may be lost.

B.: The 'I' thought is the ego and that is lost. The real 'I' is 'I am that I am.'[1]

'The doctrine of the Trinity was explained: God the Father is equivalent to Ishwara, God the Son to the Guru, and God the Holy Ghost to the Atman. *Isvaro gururatmeti murti bheda vibhagina vyomavad vyapta dehaya dakshinamurtaye namah,* means that God appears to His devotee in the form of a Guru (Son of God) and points out to him the immanence of the Holy Spirit. That is to say, that God is Spirit, that this Spirit is immanent everywhere and that the Self must be realized, which is the same as realizing God.'[2]

[1] T., p. 164 [2] T., p. 90

He protested against being satisfied with formal heavens, whether Hindu or any other, because so long as there is form there remain seer, sight and seen and not the One Self.

D.: There is a short account of the spiritual experiences of St. Theresa, in the March number of *Prabudha Bharata.* She was devoted to a figure of the Madonna which became animated to her sight and she was in bliss. Is this the same as *saktipada?*

B.: The animated figure indicates the depth of meditation (*dhyana bala*). *Saktipada* prepares the mind for introversion. There is a process of concentration of the mind on one's own shadow which in due course becomes animated and answers questions put to it. That is due to strength of mind or depth of meditation. Whatever is external is also transitory. Such phenomena may produce joy for the time being, but abiding peace (*shanti*) does not result. That is got only by the removal of *avidya* (ignorance).[1]

D.: Can't we see God in concrete form?

B.: Yes. God is seen in the mind. A concrete form may be seen but still it is only in the devotee's mind. The form and appearance in which God manifests are determined by the mind of the devotee. But that is not the ultimate experience. There is a sense of duality in it. It is like a dream or vision. After God is perceived Self-enquiry begins and that leads to Realization of the Self. Self-enquiry is the ultimate route.'[2]

Sometimes his answers were cryptic and epigrammatical. The same universal truth is to be found in them; their rather prickly form may reflect the aggressive manner of the questioner.

Q.: What is the best of all religions? What is Bhagavan's method?

B.: All methods and religions are the same.

Q.: But different methods are taught for attaining liberation.

[1] T., p. 393 [2] T., p. 251

B.: Why should you be liberated? Why not remain as you are now?

Q.: I want to get rid of pain. To be rid of pain is said to be liberation.

B.: That is what all religions teach.

Q.: But what is the method?

B.: Go back the way you came.[1]

Q.: Where did I come from?

B.: That is just what you have to find out. Did these questions arise when you were asleep? And yet you existed then. Were you not the same person?

Q.: Yes, I existed in sleep. So did the mind. But the senses had merged so that I could not speak.

B.: Are you the individual? Are you the mind? Did the mind announce itself to you when you were asleep?

Q.: No. But the authorities say that the individuality is different from God.

B.: Never mind about God; speak for yourself.

Q.: What about myself? Who am I?

B.: That is just what you have to find out. Then you will know everything. If you do not, it will be time enough to ask then.

Q.: When I wake I see the world and I am not changed at all.

B.: But you do not know this when asleep. And yet you exist in both states. Who has changed now? Is it your nature to change or to remain unchanging?

Q.: What is the proof?

B.: Does one require proof of one's own being? Only remain aware of yourself and all else will be known.

Q.: Whey then do the dualists and non-dualists quarrel among themselves?

B.: If each would attend to his own business (of seeking Realization) there would be no quarrel.[2]

---

[1] *Cf.* Christ's injunction to return to the mother's womb and be born again.
[2] T., p. 479

Spiritual experiences may be differently expressed because some form must be given to the Formless in order to express them at all, but essentially they are the same.

D.: Is the experience of the highest state the same to all, or is there any difference?

B.: The highest state is the same and the experience is the same.

D.: But I find some difference in the interpretations given of the highest truth.

B.: The interpretations are made with the mind. The minds are different, so the interpretations also differ.

D.: I mean to say that the seers express themselves differently.

B.: Their modes of expression may differ according to the nature of the seekers for whose guidance they are intended.

D.: One speaks in terms of Christianity, another of Islam, a third of Buddhism, etc. Is that due to their upbringing?

B.: Whatever may be their upbringing, their experience is the same. Only the modes of expression differ according to circumstances.[1]

So also with different paths or schools within a religion.

D.: Different teachers have set up different schools and proclaimed different truths and so confused people. Why?

B.: They have all taught the same truth but from different standpoints. Such differences were necessary to meet the needs of different minds differently constituted, but they all reveal the same truth.

D.: Since they have recommended different paths, which is one to follow?

B.: You speak of paths as if you were somewhere and the Self somewhere else and you had to go and attain it. But in fact the Self is here and now and you are it always. It is like being here and asking people the way to Ramanasramam and then

[1] T., p. 595

complaining that each one shows a different path and asking which to follow.[1]

While confirming the various religions, Bhagavan at the same time urged people to get beyond them to the One Self. Paul Brunton, author of *A Search In Secret India*, asked him about the various doctrines of heaven and hell.

D.: Why do religions speak of gods, heaven, hell, etc.?

B.: Only to make people realize that they are on a par with this world and that the Self alone is real. The religions are according to the viewpoint of the seeker. (Take the *Bhagavad Gita* for instance; when Arjuna said that he would not fight against his own relations and elders, in order to kill them and gain the kingdom, Sri Krishna said: 'Not that these, you or I were not before, are not now, nor will be hereafter. None was born, none has died, nor will it be so hereafter,' and so on. Later, as he developed the theme and declared that He had given the same instruction to the Sun, through him to Ikshvaku, etc., Arjuna raised the doubt: 'How can that be? You were born a few years ago. They lived ages ago.' Then Sri Krishna, understanding Arjuna's standpoint, said: 'Yes, there have been many incarnations of myself and yourself; I know them all, but you do not.') Such statements appear contradictory, but still both are right according to the point of view of the questioner. Christ also declared that He was even before Abraham.

D.: What is the purpose of such descriptions in religion?

B.: Only to establish the reality of the Self.

D.: Bhagavan always speaks from the highest standpoint.

B. (smiling): People will not understand the bare and simple truth—the truth of their everyday, ever present and eternal experience. That is the truth of the Self. Is there any one not aware of the Self? Yet, they do not even like to hear of it, whereas they are eager to know what lies beyond—heaven and hell and reincarnation. Because they love mystery and not the plain

[1] D.D., I, p. 61

truth, religions pamper them—only to bring them round to the Self in the end. Moreover, much as you may wander you must return ultimately to the Self, so why not abide in the Self here and now?'[1]

A passage was quoted above in which the questioner was recommended to read the Gita or the Bible constantly; and yet on other occasions people were reminded that their scriptures also have to be superseded.

'All the scriptures are meant only to make a man retrace his steps to his original source. He need not acquire anything new. He only has to give up false ideas and useless accretions. Instead of doing this, however, he tries to grasp something strange and mysterious because he believes his happiness lies elsewhere. That is the mistake.'[2]

'All scriptures without exception proclaim that for attaining salvation, the mind should be subdued. And once one knows that control of the mind is their final aim, it is futile to make an interminable study of them. What is required for such control is actual enquiry into oneself by self-interrogation: "Who am I?" How can this enquiry in quest of the Self be made by means of a study of the scriptures?

'One should realize the Self by the Eye of Wisdom. Does Rama need a mirror to recognize himself as Rama? That to which "I" refers is within the five sheaths, whereas the scriptures are outside them. Therefore, it is futile to seek by means of the study of the scriptures, the Self that has to be realized by summarily rejecting even the five sheaths.

'To enquire Who am I that is in bondage? and to know one's real nature alone is Liberation. To keep the mind constantly turned within and to abide thus in the Self is alone *Atmavichara* (Self-enquiry), whereas *dhyana* (meditation) consists in fervent contemplation of the Self as *Sat-Chit-Ananda* (Being-Con-

---

[1] T., p. 145   [2] T., p. 252

sciousness-Bliss). Indeed, at some time, one will have to forget everything that has been learnt.[1]

'The Realized Man stands forth as That to which all the attributes enumerated by the scriptures refer. To him, therefore, these sacred texts are of no use whatever.'[2]

[1] W., p. 46   [2] S.I., p. 32

2

FROM THEORY TO PRACTICE

As was shown in the previous chapter, the theory that the Maharshi taught was intended only to serve as a basis for practice. However, the demand for practice brought in another branch of theory, that of free-will or predestination, since there were not lacking people who asked why they should make any effort if everything is predestined, or if all men return to their Source in any case.

'A visitor from Bengal said: "Shankara says that we are all free, not bound, and that we shall all return to God from whom we came, like sparks from a fire. If that is so, why should we not commit all sorts of sins?"

Bhagavan's reply showed him that that cannot be the point of view of the ego.

B.: It is true that we are not bound. That is to say, the real Self has no bondage. And it is true that you will eventually return to your Source. But meanwhile, if you commit sins, as you call them, you have to face the consequences. You cannot escape them. If a man beats you, can you say: 'I am free, I am not affected by the beating and feel no pain. Let him continue beating'? If you can really feel that, then you can do what you like, but what is the use of just saying in words that you are free?[1]

Bhagavan did sometimes make pronouncements which seemed superficially like affirmations of complete predestination. When he left

[1] D.D., II, p. 254

home in his youth, already established in Self-realization, his mother sought and at last found him. He was maintaining silence at that time; therefore, on her request to return home with her, he wrote out his reply instead of replying verbally:

'The Ordainer controls the fate of souls in accordance with their *prarabdhakarma* (destiny to be worked out in this life, resulting from the balance sheet of actions in past lives). Whatever is destined not to happen will not happen, try as you may. Whatever is destined to happen will happen, do what you may to prevent it. This is certain. The best course, therefore, is to remain silent.'[1]

He sometimes also made such statements to devotees.

'All the activities that the body is to go through are determined when it first comes into existence. It does not rest with you to accept or reject them. The only freedom you have is to turn your mind inward and renounce activities there.'[2]

'With reference to Bhagavan's reply to Mrs. Desai on the evening of January 3rd, I asked him: Are only the important events in a man's life, such as his main occupation or profession, predetermined, or are trifling acts also, such as taking a cup of water or moving from one part of the room to another?'

B.: Everything is predetermined.

I.: Then what responsibility, what free will has man?

B.: Why does the body come into existence? It is designed for the various things that are marked out for it in this life. . . . As for freedom, a man is always free not to identify himself with the body and not be affected by the pleasures and pains consequent on its activities.[3]

Actually, however, the question of free will or predestination does not arise at all from the point of view of non-duality. It is as though a

[1] R.M., p. 42   [2] D.D., I, p. 32   [3] D.D., II, p. 99

group of people who had never heard of radio were to stand round a wireless set arguing whether the man in the box has to sing what the transmitting station tells him to or whether he can change parts of the songs. The answer is that there is no man in the box and therefore the question does not arise. Similarly, the answer to the question whether the ego has free will or not is that there is no ego and therefore the question does not arise. Therefore Bhagavan's usual response to the question would be to bid the questioner find out who it is that has free will or predestination.

D.: Has man any free will or is everything in his life pre-determined?'

The same question as above, but the answer differs according to the needs of the questioner. In fact, if one does not bear in mind what has just been said about the unreality of the ego it seems to be quite contradictory.

B.: Free will exists together with the individuality. As long as the individuality lasts, so long is there free will. All the scriptures are based on this fact and advise directing the free will in the right channel.

Is this really a contradiction of the reply given earlier? No, because, according to Bhagavan's teaching, the individuality has only an illusory existence. So long as one imagines that one has a separate individuality, so long does one also imagine its free will. The two exist together inevitably. The problem of predestination and free will has always plagued philosophers and theologians and will always continue to do so, because it is insoluble on the plane of duality, that is on the supposition of one being who is the Creator and a lot of other, separate beings who are created. If they have free will, then he is not omnipotent and omniscient—he does not know what will happen, because it depends on what they decide; and he cannot control all happenings because they have the power to change them. On the other hand, if he is omniscient and omnipotent he has fore-knowledge of all that will happen and controls everything, and therefore they can have no power of decision, that is to say no free will. But on the level of advaita or non-duality the problem fades out and ceases to exist. In truth the ego has no free will, because there is no ego; but on the level of apparent reality the ego consists of free will—it is the illusion of free will that creates the illusion of the ego. That is what Bhagavan meant by saying that 'as long as the individuality lasts, so long is there free will'. The next sentence in his answer turns the questioner away from theory to practice.

'Find out who it is who has free will or predestination and abide in that state. Then both are transcended. That is the only purpose in discussing these questions. To whom do such questions present themselves? Discover that and be at peace.[1]

'The only path of karma (action), *bhakti* (devotion), yoga and *jnana* (knowledge) is to enquire who it is who has the karma, *vibhakti* (lack of devotion), *viyoga* (separation) and *ajnana* (ignorance). Through this investigation, the ego disappears and the state of abidance in the Self in which none of these negative qualities ever existed, remains as the Truth.[2]

'As long as a man is the doer he also reaps the fruits of his deeds, but as soon as he realizes the Self through enquiry as to who is the doer, his sense of being the doer falls away and the triple karma (destiny) is ended. This is the state of eternal liberation.'[3]

Bhagavan said: 'We are all really *Sat-chit-ananda* (Being-Knowledge-Bliss) but we imagine that we are bound (by destiny) and have all this suffering.'

I asked him why we imagine this, why this state of ignorance (*ajnana*) comes over us.

Bhagavan said: 'Ask yourself to whom this ignorance has come and you will discover that it never came to you and that you always have been *Sat-chit-ananda*. One goes through all sorts of austerities to become what one already is. All effort is

[1] T., p. 426 [2] F.V.S., p. 79 [3] F.V., p. 76

simply to get rid of the mistaken impression that one is limited and bound by the woes of *samsara* (this life).'[1]

D.: Is there predestination? And if what is destined to happen will happen, is there any use in prayer or effort or should we just remain idle?

This is a concise form of the question which Bhagavan was so often asked, and the reply is typical in that it does not expound theory but prescribes what to do.

B.: There are only two ways in which to conquer destiny or be independent of it. One is to enquire who undergoes this destiny and discover that only the ego is bound by it and not the Self, and that the ego is non-existent. The other way is to kill the ego by completely surrendering to the Lord, by realizing one's helplessness and saying all the time: 'Not I, but Thou, O my Lord', and giving up all sense of 'I' and 'mine' and leaving it to the Lord to do what he likes with you. Surrender can never be regarded as complete so long as the devotee wants this or that from the Lord. True surrender is love of God for the sake of love and for nothing else, not even for the sake of salvation. In other words, complete effacement of the ego is necessary to conquer destiny, whether you achieve this effacement through Self-enquiry or through *bhakti-marga*.[2]

This mode of reply is common to spiritual teachers. I remember once reading the life of a Sufi saint, Abu Said, by Professor Nicholson, in which the learned author concluded that he seems to have taught predestination in theory but free will in practice. Puzzling as it may be for the philosopher, this is the attitude of all spiritual teachers, just as Christ affirmed that not even a sparrow can fall without the will of God, and that the very hairs on one's head are numbered, just as the Quran affirms that all knowledge and power are with God and that He leads aright whom He will and leads astray whom He will; and yet both Christ and the Quran exhort men to right effort and condemn

[1] D.D., II, p. 53   [2] D.D., I, p. 57

sin. Bhagavan was quite categorical that effort is necessary. In actual life everyone realizes this, whatever theoretical view he may hold. A man makes the physical effort of putting the food in his mouth and eating; he does not say: What is the use of eating if I am predestined to die of starvation? He makes the mental effort of earning the money to buy food to eat. Why should he, then, apply a different logic when it comes to spiritual effort?

'A young man from Colombo, Ceylon, said to Bhagavan: "J. Krishnamurthi teaches the method of effortless and choiceless awareness as distinct from that of deliberate concentration. Would Sri Bhagavan be pleased to explain how best to practise meditation and what form the object of meditation shall take?"'

B.: Effortless and choiceless awareness is our real nature. If we can attain that state and abide in it, that is all right. But one cannot reach it without effort, the effort of deliberate meditation. All the age-old *vasanas* (inherent tendencies) turn the mind outwards to external objects. All such thoughts have to be given up and the mind turned inwards and that, for most people, requires effort. Of course, every teacher and every book tells the aspirant to keep quiet, but it is not easy to do so. That is why all this effort is necessary. Even if we find somebody who has achieved this supreme state of stillness, you may take it that the necessary effort had already been made in a previous life. So, effortless and choiceless awareness is attained only after deliberate meditation. That meditation can take whatever form most appeals to you. See what helps you to keep out all other thoughts and adopt that for your meditation.

'In this connection Bhagavan quoted some verses from the great Tamil poet and saint Thayumanavar, the gist of which is as follows: Bliss will ensue if you keep still, but however much you tell your mind this truth, it will not keep still. It is the mind that tells the mind to be still and it will attain bliss, but it will not do it. Though all the scriptures have said it and though we hear it daily from the great ones and even from our Guru, we are never quiet but stray into the world of *Maya* (illusion) and sense objects. That is why conscious, deliberate effort is needed to attain that effortless state of stillness.'[1]

Indeed, until the supreme, effortless state is attained, it is impossible for a man not to make effort. His own nature compels him to, just as Sri Krishna in the Bhagavad Gita, told Arjuna that his own nature would compel him to fight.

D.: I want to be further enlightened. Should I try to make no effort at all?

B.: Now it is impossible for you to be without effort. When you go deeper, it is impossible for you to make effort.[2]

D.: What is the difference between meditation and *samadhi* or absorption in the Self?

B.: Meditation is initiated and sustained by a conscious effort of the mind. When such effort entirely subsides, it is called *samadhi*.[3]

B.: If you can keep still without engaging in any other pursuits, well and good. But if that cannot be done, what is the use of remaining inactive only with regard to realization? So long as you are obliged to be active, do not give up the attempt to realize the Self.[4]

'Meditation is a fight. As soon as you begin meditation, other thoughts will crowd together, gather force and try to overwhelm the single thought to which you try to hold. This thought must gradually gain strength by repeated practice. When it has grown strong, the other thoughts will be put to flight. This is the battle always going on in meditation.[5]

'So long as the ego lasts, effort is necessary. When the ego ceases to exist, actions become spontaneous.[6]

'No one succeeds without effort. Mind control is not your

[1] D.D., II, p. 112   [2] S.D.B., IV   [3] S.I., p. 34   [4] T., p. 255   [5] T., p. 371   [6] T., p. 467

birthright. The few who succeed owe their success to their perseverance.'[1]

Sometimes glimpses of Realization are attained before it becomes permanent, and in such cases effort still continues to be necessary.

'Effort is necessary up to the state of Realization. Even then, the Self should spontaneously become evident; otherwise happiness will not be complete. Up to that state of spontaneity there must be effort in some form or another.'[2]

Sometimes right effort is referred to as a duty.

D.: Why should I try to get Realization? I shall emerge from this state of illusion just as I wake up from a dream. We do not make any effort to get out of a dream when we are asleep.

B.: In a dream you have no inkling that it is a dream and therefore no obligation to make an effort to get out of it. But in this life you have some intuition based on your experience of sleep and on what you hear and read, that it is a sort of dream, and this intuition imposes on you the duty of making an effort to get out of it. However, who wants to realize the Self if you don't want to? If you prefer to be in this dream, stay as you are.[3]

Sometimes, however, as in the following very similar conversation, the seeker was reminded that even the effort is a part of the illusion of individual being.

D.: It is said that our waking life is also a dream, similar to our dream during sleep. But in our dreams we make no conscious effort to get rid of the dream and to wake up; the dream itself comes to an end without any effort on our part and we become awake. Similarly, why shouldn't the waking state, which in reality is only another sort of dream, come to an end of its own accord, without any effort on our part, and land us in Realization or real awakening?

[1] T., p. 398   [2] T., p. 78   [3] D.D., II, p. 97

B.: Your thinking that you have to make an effort to get rid of this dream of a waking state and your making efforts to attain Realization or real awakening are all parts of the dream. When you attain Realization you will see there was neither the dream during sleep nor the waking state, but only yourself and your real state.[1]

Sometimes the question took the form of apparent conflict not between effort and destiny but between effort and grace, for there were those who asked what use effort was if Realization was dependent on the grace of God or Guru. In one form or another this doubt tends to arise in any religion, as in the Christian dispute whether salvation is due to grace or good works. Really, as the following quotations show, there is no conflict between the two.

V.: It is said that only those who are chosen for Self-realization obtain it. That is rather discouraging.

B.: That only means that we cannot attain realization of the Self by our own mind, unaided by God's grace.

'I interposed: Bhagavan also says that even that grace does not come arbitrarily but because one has deserved it by one's own efforts either in this life or in previous ones.'

V.: But human effort is said to be useless; so what incentive has a man to improve himself?

'I asked where it was said that you should make no effort or that effort was useless; and the visitor pointed to the passage in "Who am I?" where it says that, since the indefinable power of the Lord ordains, sustains and controls everything, we need not worry what we shall do.[2] I pointed out that what is deprecated there is not human effort but the feeling "I am the doer". I asked Bhagavan whether my explanation was not right and he approved of it.'[3]

D.: Grace is necessary for the removal of ignorance.

B.: Certainly. But Grace is there all along. Grace is the Self. It is not something to be acquired. All that is necessary is to know its existence. In the same way, the sun is pure brightness; it does

[1] D.D., II, p. 17 [2] W., p. 45 [3] D.D., II, p. 4

not know darkness, although others speak of darkness fleeing away on its approach. Like darkness, ignorance is a phantom, not real. Because of its unreality, it is said to be removed when its unreality is discovered.

'The sun is there and shines and you are surrounded by sunlight; still, if you would know the sun you must turn your eyes in its direction and look at it. Similarly, Grace is only to be found by effort, although it is here and now.'

D.: By the desire to surrender, increasing grace is experienced, I hope?

B.: Surrender once and for all and be done with the desire. So long as the sense of being the doer remains desire does also. Therefore the ego remains. But once this goes the Self shines forth in its purity. The sense of being the doer is the bondage, not the actions themselves. 'Be still and know that I am God.' Here stillness is total surrender without a vestige of individuality. Stillness will prevail and there will be no agitation of the mind. Agitation of mind is the cause of desire, of the sense of being the doer, of personality. If that is stopped, there is quiet. In this sense, 'knowing' means 'being'. It is not relative knowledge involving the triads of knower, knowledge and known.[1]

D.: But one may not be quite sure of God's grace?

B.: If the unripe mind does not feel God's grace, it does not mean that this is absent, for that would imply that God is at times not gracious, that is to say ceases to be God.

D.: Is that the same as the saying of Christ: According to thy faith be it done unto thee?

B.: Quite so.

D.: The Upanishads say, I am told, that he alone knows the Atman whom the Atman chooses. Why should the Atman choose at all? If it chooses, why some particular person?

B.: When the sun rises some buds blossom, not all. Do you blame the sun for that? Nor can the bud blossom of itself, it requires the sunlight to enable it to do so.

[1] T., p. 354

D.: May we not say that the help of the Atman is needed because it is the Atman that drew over itself the veil of *Maya?*

B.: You may say so.

D.: If the Atman has drawn the veil over itself, should it not itself remove the veil?

B.: It will. But who complains of being veiled? Ask yourself that.

D.: Why should I? Let the Atman itself remove the veil.

B.: If the Atman complains about the veil, then the Atman will remove it.[1]

D.: If the Supreme Being is omnipresent, as He is said to be, His realization ought to be an easy thing. The scriptures, however, declare that without His grace the Lord cannot even be worshipped, much less realized. So then, how can the individual by his own effort realize the Self, or the Supreme Being, except through His grace?

B.: There was never a time when the Supreme Being was unknown or unrealized, because He is one and identical with the Self. His grace or *Anugraha* is the same as the conscious immediacy of His Divine Presence, *Prasannata,* in other words, Enlightenment or Revelation. One's ignorance of this self-revealing immediacy of Divine Grace is no proof to the contrary. If the owl does not see the sun that illumines the whole world, is that the fault of the sun? Is it not due to the defectiveness of the bird's sight? Similarly, if the ignorant man is unaware of the everluminous Atman or Self, can that be attributed to the nature of the Atman itself? Is it not the result of his own ignorance? The Supreme Lord is eternal grace. Therefore, there is really no such individual act as bestowing Grace; and, being ever present, the manifestation of Grace is not confined to any particular period or occasion.[2]

Turning to God and desiring His grace is itself grace.

[1] M.G., p. 54   [2] S.I., p. 24

D.: Doubts keep arising. That is why I ask how it is to be done.

B.: A doubt arises and it is cleared. Another arises and that is cleared, only to make way for another, and so it goes on. So there is no possibility of clearing away all doubts. Find out instead to whom the doubts come. Go to their source and stay there. Then they cease to arise. That is how doubts are to be cleared away.

D.: Only grace can help me do it.

B.: Grace is not something outside you. In fact your very desire for grace is due to grace that is already working in you.[1]

Grace is represented alike as the grace of God or Guru.

D.: Isn't success dependent on the grace of the Guru?

B.: Yes, but isn't your practice itself due to such grace? Its fruits spring from it automatically. There is a stanza in Kaivalya which runs: 'O Guru, you have always been with me, watching over me, one incarnation after another, and have shaped my course until I was Liberated.' The Self manifests externally as the Guru when occasion demands; otherwise he always remains within, doing what is required.[2]

V.: In actual practice, I find I cannot succeed in my efforts unless Bhagavan's grace descends on me.

B.: The Guru's Grace is always there. You imagine it to be something somewhere high up in the sky that has to descend, but really it is inside you, in your heart, and the moment you effect the subsidence or merging of the mind into its Source, by whatever method, the Grace rushes forth, spouting as from a spring within you.[3]

---

[1] T., p. 618   [2] T., p. 425   [3] D.D. II, p. 31

3

LIFE IN THE WORLD

Once anyone decided to proceed from theory to practice on the basis of Bhagavan's teachings, the question was apt to arise how that affected his life in the world. Hinduism does not necessarily enjoin physical renunciation for active spiritual seekers, as did, for instance, the original teaching of Christ or Buddha. On the contrary, the state of the householder is honoured and the path of right action is a legitimate path. In fact, the classical system in ancient India was that a man should retire into the homeless state only after he had fulfilled his duties as a householder and had an adult son or sons to replace him.

However, the doctrine of non-duality, together with the path of Self-enquiry (to be described in a later chapter), which is based on it, has been traditionally recognized as suitable to the world-renouncer. It was therefore natural that Bhagavan's followers often asked him whether they should renounce the world. At the same time, it was a remarkable indication of the amount of spiritual determination which still remains in modern India, for renouncing the world does not mean living a solitary life in a little house and garden of one's own, as it might in the West, or even retiring to the austere security of a monastery, but going forth homeless and penniless, depending on the charitable for food and clothing and sleeping in a cave or temple or wherever possible. It does sometimes happen in modern times that a sadhu accepts a small grant from his family—enough to buy food and the simplest clothing; but even so, it is a bare, hard life. Nevertheless, there were constant requests to be allowed to take this life and constantly Bhagavan withheld permission. The work was internal and had to be done in the mind, whatever the conditions of life.

B.: Why do you think you are a householder? The similar thought that you are a *sannyasi* will haunt you even if you go forth as one. Whether you continue in the household or renounce it and go to live in the forest, your mind haunts you. The ego is the source of thought. It creates the body and the world and makes you think of being a householder. If you renounce, it will only substitute the thought of renunciation for that of the family and the environment of the forest for that of the household. But the mental obstacles are always there for you. They even increase greatly in the new surroundings. Change of environment is no help. The one obstacle is the mind, and this must be overcome whether in the home or in the forest. If you can do it in the forest, why not in the home? So why change the environment? Your efforts can be made even now, whatever be the environment.

D.: Is it possible to enjoy *samadhi* while busy with worldly work?

B.: It is the feeling 'I work' that is the hindrance. Ask yourself: 'Who works?' Remember who you are. Then the work will not bind you. It will go on automatically. Make no effort either to work or to renounce; your effort is the bondage. What is destined to happen will happen. If you are destined to work, you will not be able to avoid it; you will be forced to engage in it. So leave it to the Higher Power. It is not really your choice whether you renounce or retain.[1]

'When women carrying jars of water on their heads stop to talk, they are very careful, keeping their mind on the water jars. Similarly, when a sage engages in activity, his mind remains fixed in the Self and his activity does not distract him.'[2]

D.: I believe celibacy is necessary even for a householder if he is to succeed in Self-enquiry. Am I right?

B.: First find out who the wife and husband are. Then the question will not arise.

[1] M.G., I, p. 6   [2] T., p. 231

D.: Isn't Brahmacharya (celibacy) necessary for realization of the Self?

B.: Brahmacharya means 'living in Brahman'; it has no connection with celibacy as commonly understood. A real Brahmachari is one who lives in Brahman and finds bliss in Brahman, which is the same as the Self. Why, then, should he look for other sources of happiness? In fact, it is emergence from the Self that is the cause of all misery.

D.: But isn't celibacy necessary for yoga?

B.: It is one aid to realization among many others.

D.: Then is it not indispensable? Can a married man realize the Self?

B.: Certainly. It is a question of fitness of mind. Married or unmarried, a man can realize the Self, because the Self is here and now. If it were not, but were obtainable by some effort at some future time, if it were something new to be acquired, it would not be worth seeking, because what is not natural cannot be permanent. What I say is that the Self is here and now and that IT alone is.[1]

D.: Is it necessary to take *sannyasa* (a vow of renunciation) in order to attain Self-realization?

B.: Sannyasa means renouncing one's individuality, not shaving one's head and putting on ochre robes. A man may be a householder but if he does not think he is one he is a *sannyasin*. On the other hand, he may wear ochre robes and wander about, but so long as he thinks he is a *sannyasin* he is not one. To think about one's renunciation defeats the purpose of renouncing.[2]

'What do you mean by taking *sannyasa?* Do you think it means leaving your home or wearing robes of a certain colour? Wherever you go, even if you fly up into the air, will your mind not go with you? Or, can you leave it behind you and go without it?[3]

'Why should your occupation or duties in life interfere with your spiritual effort? For instance, there is a difference between your activities at home and in the office. In your office activities,

[1] T., p. 17   [2] T., p. 427   [3] D.D., I, p. 15

you are detached and so long as you do your duty you do not care what happens or whether it results in gain or loss to the employer. Your duties at home, on the other hand, are performed with attachment and you are all the time anxious whether they will bring advantage to you and your family. But it is possible to perform all the activities of life with detachment and regard only the Self as real. It is wrong to suppose that if one is fixed in the Self, one's duties in life will not be properly performed. It is like an actor. He dresses and acts and even feels the part he is playing, but he knows really that he is not that character but someone else in real life. In the same way, why should the body consciousness or the feeling 'I-am-the-body' disturb you, once you know for certain that you are not the body but the Self? Nothing that the body does should shake you from abidance in the Self. Such abidance will never interfere with the proper and effective discharge of whatever duties the body has, any more than an actor's being aware of his real status in life interferes with his acting a part on the stage.'[1]

D.: It has been definitely stated that so long as there is the least trace of the 'I-am-the-doer' idea there can be no realization, but is it possible for a householder who earnestly desires Liberation to fulfil his duties without this idea?

B.: There is no principle that actions can be performed only on the basis of the 'I-am-the-doer' idea, and therefore there is no reason to ask whether they can be performed and the duties discharged without that idea. To take a common example, an accountant working all day in his office and scrupulously attending to his duties might seem to the spectator to be shouldering all the financial responsibilities of the institution. But, knowing that he is not personally affected by the in-take or out-goings, he remains unattached and free from the 'I-am-the-doer' feeling in doing his work, while at the same time he does it perfectly well. In the same way, it is quite possible for the wise householder who earnestly seeks liberation to discharge his duties in life (which,

[1] D.D., I, p. 31

after all, are his destiny) without any attachment, regarding himself merely as an instrument for the purpose. Such activity is not an obstacle on the path to Knowledge nor does Knowledge prevent a man from discharging his duties in life. Knowledge and activity are never mutually antagonistic and the realization of one does not impede performance of the other, nor performance of one the realization of the other.

D.: What is the significance of the life of a spiritually minded householder who has to devote all his time merely to earning a living and supporting his family and what mutual benefit do they get?

B.: The discharge of his duties by a householder such as this, who works for the support of his family, quite unmindful of his own physical comforts in life, should be regarded as selfless service rendered to his family, whose needs it is his destiny to meet. It may, however, be asked what benefit such a householder derives from the family..The answer is that there is no benefit for him from the family as such, since he has made the discharge of his duties to them a means of spiritual training and since he finally obtains perfect contentment by realizing the supreme Bliss of Liberation, which is the ultimate goal of every path and the supreme reward. He therefore stands in need of nothing from the members of his family or from his family life.

D.: How can a householder who is constantly engaged in the active discharge of his domestic duties, which should naturally impel him to still greater activity, obtain the supreme peace of withdrawal and freedom from the urge to such activity even while thus busily engaged?

B.: It is only to the spectator that the enlightened householder seems to be occupied with his domestic duties; for even though apparently engaged in domestic duties, he is not really engaged in any activity at all. His outer activity does not prevent him from realizing the perfect peace of withdrawal, and he is free from the restless urge to activity even in the midst of his activities.[1]

[1] S.I., p. 23

Visitor: Should I retire from business and take to reading books on Vedanta?

B.: If objects have an independent existence, that is if they exist somewhere apart from you, then it may be possible for you to retire from them. But they do not. They owe their existence to you, to your thought, so where can you retire from them? As for reading books on Vedanta, you can go on reading any number but they can only tell you to realize the Self within you. The Self cannot be found in books. You have to find it for yourself in yourself.[1]

D.: Is a vow of silence useful?

B.: The inner silence is self-surrender. And that means living without the sense of ego.

D.: Is solitude necessary for a *sannyasin?*

B.: Solitude is in the mind of a man. One man may be in the thick of the world and yet maintain perfect serenity of mind. Such a person is always in solitude. Another may live in the forest but still be unable to control his mind. He cannot be said to be in solitude. Solitude is an attitude of the mind. A man attached to the things of life cannot get solitude, wherever he may be, whereas a detached man is always in solitude.[2]

As this implies, Bhagavan did not approve of a vow of silence, such as people sometimes take in order to create a sort of solitude in society. The real silence, he taught, is a still mind. If the mind is active, there is no benefit in not speaking. What is needed is to control both thought and speech.

'The silence of solitude is forced. Restrained speech in society is equivalent to silence, for then a man controls his speech. There must be a speaker before there can be speech. If the mind of the speaker is engaged otherwise, speech is restrained. When the mind is turned inwards it is active in a different way and is not anxious to speak. The purpose of a vow of silence is to limit the mental activities provoked by speech, but if the mind is controlled, this is unnecessary and silence becomes natural.'[3]

[1] D.D., II, p. 1   [2] M.G., I, p. 14   [3] T., p. 60

Until the mind is ripe to do so, it is not even possible to give up activity.

D.: How does activity help? Doesn't it simply increase the already heavy load upon us that we have to get rid of?

B.: Action performed unselfishly purifies the mind and helps it to fix itself in meditation.

D.: But suppose one were to meditate constantly without activity?

B.: Try and see. Your latent tendencies will not let you. Meditation only comes gradually with their gradual weakening, by the grace of the Guru.[1]

Even in the case of one who had fulfilled his destiny as a house-holder and, having grown-up children to take his place, could have renounced the world according to the classical Indian tradition, Bhagavan still did not give his sanction.

D.: I have no pleasure in my family. There remains nothing for me to do there. I have done what had to be done and now there are grandsons and grand-daughters in the house. Should I remain there or should I leave it and go away?

B.: You should stay just where you are now. But where are you now? Are you in the house or is the house in you? Is there any house apart from you? If you become established in your own place, you will find that all things have merged into you and such questions will become unnecessary.

D.: Then it seems I am to remain at home?

B.: You are to remain in your true state.

Sometimes the Maharshi was asked why he himself renounced the world and went forth to the homeless life, if he did not approve of that path for his followers, and he replied merely that such was his destiny. It is to be remembered that the path he taught, the use of Self-enquiry in the life of the world, combined with harmonious action, is a new path created by him to meet the needs of our time. He himself had to be established in Realization before he could establish the path thereto.

[1] T., p. 80

D.: Can I engage in spiritual practice even while remaining in the life of the world?

B.: Yes, certainly; one ought to do so.

D.: Isn't life in the world a hindrance? Don't all the books advocate renunciation?

B.: The world is only in the mind. It does not speak out, saying: 'I am the world'. If it did, it would have to be always present even in your sleep. Since it is not present in sleep, it is impermanent. Being impermanent, it has no reality. Having no reality, it is easily subdued by the Self. The Self alone is permanent. Renunciation is non-identification of the Self with the non-self. On the disappearance of ignorance, the non-self ceases to exist. That is true renunciation.

D.: Why then did you leave your home in your youth?

B.: That is my *prarabdha* (destiny). One's course of conduct in this life is determined by one's *prarabdha*. My *prarabdha* lies this way; yours lies that way.

D.: Should I not also renounce?

B.: If that had been your *prarabdha*, the question would not have arisen.

D.: Then I take it that I should remain in the world and engage in spiritual practice. But if I do so can I obtain realization in this life?

B.: This has already been answered. You are always the Self. Earnest efforts never fail. Success is bound to result.[1]

With many European and some Indian visitors, it was the opposite question that arose—not whether they should renounce the world but what they could do to help it. Being 'in the world but not of it', following the inner spiritual quest while outwardly conforming to the conditions of life, seemed to them too much of a withdrawal, not too little. To some extent, Bhagavan's answers varied according to the understanding of the questioner. If the latter was capable of spiritual understanding he would turn him inwards.

D.: Why is the world enveloped in ignorance?

[1] T., p. 251

B.: Look after yourself and let the world look after itself. What is your Self? If you are the body there is a physical world also, but if you are the Spirit, there is only Spirit.[1]

Visitor: What do you think about social reform?

B.: Self-reform automatically results in social reform Attend to self-reform and social reform will take care of itself.[2]

However, people who raised this sort of objection were more often of a devotional temperament, such as requires worship and a dualistic religion; and in such cases Bhagavan would enjoin submission to God. All that is required is to submit to God and do one's duty, play one's part in life, with full confidence. That is all that is asked of one. One is not responsible for the outcome.

B.: Now, I will ask you a question. When a man gets into a train, where does he put his luggage?

D.: Either in the compartment or in the luggage van.

B.: He doesn't carry it on his head or in his lap while on the train?

D.: Only a fool would do so.

B.: It is a thousand times more foolish to bear your own burden once you have undertaken the spiritual quest, whether by the path of knowledge or devotion.

D.: But can I relinquish all my responsibilities, all my commitments?

B.: You remember the temple tower? There are many statues on it, aren't there? Well, there are four big ones at the base, one at each corner. Have you seen them?

D.: Yes.

B.: Well, I tell you that the huge tower is supported by these four statues.

D.: How is that possible? What does Bhagavan mean?

B.: I mean that to say that is no more foolish than saying that you bear all the cares, burdens and responsibilities of life. The Lord of the universe bears the whole burden. You only imagine

[1] T., p. 363 [2] T., p. 282

that you do. You can hand over all your burdens to Him. Whatever you have to do, you will be made an instrument for doing it
at the right time. Do not imagine that you cannot do it unless
you have the desire to. It is not desire that gives you the necessary
strength. The strength is the Lord's.[1]

Sometimes there was a more pressing anxiety about the state
of the world and a desire to assume responsibility.

D.: Will Maharshi give his opinion on the future of the
world, as we are living in critical times?

B.: Why should you worry about the future? You don't
even know the present properly. Take care of the present and
the future will take care of itself.

D.: Will the world soon enter a new era of friendliness and
mutual help or will it go down in chaos and war?

B.: There is One who governs the world and it is His task
to look after it. He who has given life to the world knows how to
look after it also. He bears the burden of this world, not you.

D.: Yet, if one looks round with unprejudiced eyes, it is
hard to see where this benevolent care comes in.

B.: As you are, so is the world. Without understanding
yourself, what is the use of trying to understand the world? This
is a question that seekers after Truth need not worry about.
People waste their energy over all such questions. First find out
the Truth behind yourself, then you will be in a better position
to understand the Truth behind the world of which you are a
part.[2]

'Another visitor asked Bhagavan for a benedictory foreword
to a book he had written, called *The Destiny of the World* or
something of that sort. He said that someone else had already
agreed to write an introduction but he would be grateful if Bhagavan would write a few words conveying his message and blessing.
Bhagavan explained to him that he had never done such a thing

and therefore should not be expected to now. The visitor persisted, and I went to some trouble to convince him that all his persuasion would be in vain. Then he began saying that the world badly needs a spiritual message and that the youth of India and of the world are not properly brought up, since religion is not instilled into them, and so forth. I had to tell him that Bhagavan holds that before a man tries to reform the world he should first know himself, and then he can go about reforming the world if he still feels so inclined. I believe the visitor was for continuing the argument, but fortunately it was time for the *Parayanam* (recital of the Vedas) and he was effectively stopped thereby.'[1]

D.: Should I try to help the suffering world?

B.: The Power that created you created the world as well. If God created the world it is His business to look after it, not yours.[2]

Nevertheless, this does not mean that Bhagavan's teaching condoned coldness or callousness to human suffering. Those who were in distress had to be helped; only they had to be helped in a spirit of humility. What was forbidden was only the self-importance inherent in trying to act the part of providence. This is made very clear in the following passage:

D.: But we see pain in the world. A man is hungry. It is a physical reality. It is very real to him. Are we to call it a dream and remain unmoved by his suffering?

B.: From the point of view of *jnana* or Reality, the suffering you speak of is certainly a dream, as is the world of which that suffering is an infinitesimal part. In a dream you have when you are asleep you yourself feel hunger and see others also suffering from hunger. You feed yourself and, moved by pity, feed the others who are hungry. So long as the dream lasted, all this suffering was quite as real as the suffering you see in the world

---

[1] D.D., I, p. 16   [2] M.G., I, p. 33

is to you now. It was only when you woke up that you discovered it to be unreal. You might have eaten heartily before going to sleep, but you still dreamt that you had been working hard in the hot sun all day and were tired and hungry. Then you woke up and found that your stomach was full and that you had not stirred from your bed. But all this is not to say that while you are in the dream you can act as if the suffering you feel in it is not real. The hunger in the dream has to be appeased by dream food. The fellow beings you find hungry in the dream have to be provided with dream food. You can never mix the two states, the dream and the waking state. Similarly, till you attain the state of Realization and thus wake out of this illusory, phenomenal world, you must do social service by relieving suffering whenever you see it. But even so you must do it without *ahankara*, that is without the sense of: 'It is I who am doing it'. Instead you should feel: 'I am the Lord's instrument'. Similarly you must not be conceited and think: 'I am helping a man who is below me. He needs help and I am in a position to give it. I am superior and he is inferior.' You must help him as a means of worshipping God in him. All such service is serving the Self, not anybody else. You are not helping anybody else, but only yourself.[1]

In general, Bhagavan discouraged political activity among those dedicated to the quest.

D.: Is it not our duty to be patriots?

B.: It is your duty to BE and not to be this or that. 'I am that I am' sums up the whole of the Truth. The method is summarized in 'Be still.'[2]

However, when people who were engaged in political life approached him, he would simply advise them to carry on in a spirit of service and surrender, seeking to eliminate all egoism from their work.

[1] D.D., II, p. 102   [2] M.G., I, p. 33

D.: Is the desire for *swaraj* (independence) right?

B.: Such desire no doubt begins with self-interest. Yet practical work for the goal gradually widens the outlook so that the individual becomes merged in the country. Such merging of the individuality is desirable and the karma in question is *nishkāma* (unselfish).

D.: If self-government for India is granted after a long struggle and terrible sacrifice, is one not justified in being pleased with the result and elated by it?

B.: In the course of one's work one must have surrendered oneself to the higher Power whose might must be kept in mind and never lost sight of. How then can one be elated? One should not even care for the result of one's action. Then alone the karma becomes unselfish.[1]

B.: Gandhiji has surrendered himself to the Divine and works accordingly with no self interest. He does not concern himself with the results but accepts them as they turn up. That must be the attitude of national workers.

Q.: Will the work be crowned with success?

B.: This question arises because the questioner has not surrendered himself.

Q.: Should we then not think of and work for the welfare of the country?

B.: First take care of yourself and the rest will naturally follow.

Q.: I am not speaking individually but for the country.

B.: First surrender and then see. Doubts arise because of the absence of surrender. Acquire strength by surrender and then your surroundings will be found to have improved to the degree of strength acquired by you.[2]

Persons whose temperament drew them to activity and who found it hard to understand that spiritually there are no others, queried whether there was not some egoism in seeking their own realization,

[1] T., p. 502 [2] T., p. 521

not understanding that the very expression 'their own' did not apply and that not merely egoism but the ego itself had to be renounced. Bhagavan himself was asked why he did not go about preaching to the people.

D.: Why doesn't Sri Bhagavan go about preaching the truth to the people at large?

B.: How do you know that I don't? Does preaching consist in mounting a platform and haranguing the people around? Preaching is simple communication of knowledge and can be done in silence too. What do you think of a man listening to a harangue for an hour and going away without being impressed by it so as to change his life? Compare him with another who sits in a holy presence and leaves after some time with his outlook on life totally changed. Which is better: to preach loudly without effect or to sit silently sending forth intuitive force to act on others? Again, how does speech arise? First, there is abstract knowledge (unmanifest). From this there arises the ego which gives rise to thoughts and words successively. So then:

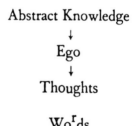

Abstract Knowledge

↓

Ego

↓

Thoughts

Wo^rds

Words therefore are the great-grandsons of the original source. If words can produce an effect, consider how much more powerful preaching through silence must be.[1]

Bhagavan answered those who doubted its utility that Realization was the greatest help they could possibly render to others. Indeed, Bhagavan himself was the standing proof of this, as one saw from the

[1] T., p. 285

numbers of people helped to the very depth of their being, lifted out of confusion and sorrow on to a firm path of peace and understanding, by the silent influence of his grace. And yet, at the same time, he reminded them that, from the point of view of knowledge, there are no others to help.

D.: Does my Realization help others?

B.: Yes, certainly. It is the best possible help. But really there are no others to help, for a Realized Being sees only the Self just as a goldsmith, estimating the gold in various jewels, sees only the gold. Separate forms and beings exist only as long as you identify yourself with the body. When you transcend the body, others disappear along with your body-consciousness.

D.: Is it so with plants, trees and so on also?

B.: Do they exist at all apart from the Self? Find out. You think that you see them. The thought is projected from yourself. Find out wherefrom it arises. The thoughts will cease to rise and the Self alone will remain.

D.: I understand theoretically, but they are still there.

B.: Yes, it is like a cinema show. There is the light on the screen and the shadows flitting across impress the audience as the acting of some story. Now suppose that in this film story an audience is also shown on the screen. The seer and the seen will then both be on the screen. Apply this to yourself. You are the screen, the Self has created the ego, the ego has its accretions of thoughts, which are displayed as the world, trees, plants, etc., about which you are asking. In reality all these are nothing but the Self. If you see the Self it will be found to be all, everywhere and always. Nothing but the Self exists.[1]

The same was explained to Mr. Evans-Wentz, the well-known writer about Tibet.

E.W.: They say that there are many saints in Tibet who remain in solitude and are still very helpful to the world. How can that be?

[1] T., p. 13

B.: It can be so. Realization of the Self is the greatest help that can be rendered to humanity. Therefore saints are said to be helpful even though they remain in the forests. But it should not be forgotten that solitude is not to be found in forests only. It can be had even in towns in the thick of worldly occupation.

E.W.: Isn't it necessary that saints should mix with people and be helpful to them?

B.: The Self alone is the Reality; the world and the rest of it are not. The Realized Being does not see the world as different from himself.

E.W.: Then does that mean that a man's Realization leads to the uplift of mankind without their being aware of it?

B.: Yes; the help is imperceptible but is still there. A Realized Man helps the whole of mankind although without their knowledge.

E.W.: Wouldn't it be better if he mixed with others?

B.: There are no others to mix with. The Self is the one and only Reality.

E.W.: If there were a hundred Self-realized men, wouldn't it be to the greater benefit of the world?

B.: When you say 'Self' you refer to the unlimited, but when you add 'men' to it, you limit the meaning. There is only one Infinite Self.

E.W.: Yes, I see. Sri Krishna has said in the Gita that work must be performed without attachment and such work is better than idleness. Is that Karma Yoga?

B.: What is said is adapted to the temperament of the listener.

E.W.: In Europe people do not understand that a man can be helpful in solitude. They imagine that only men who work in the world can be useful. When will this confusion cease? Will the European mind continue wading in the morass or will it realize the Truth?

B.: Never mind about Europe or America. Where are they but in the mind? Realize your Self and then all is realized. If you see a number of men in a dream and then wake up and recall your dream, do you try to find out whether the persons of your dream-creation are also awake?[1]

'A self-realized being cannot help benefiting the world. His very existence is the highest good.'[2]

[1] T., p. 20 [2] T., p. 210

4

THE GURU

It has always been taught that in order to attain Realization not only practice but also a guide is needed. In this, as in all things, Bhagavan gave the doctrine its deepest meaning. In fact, it became essentially the same as the Christian doctrine of 'the Christ in you' or the Buddhist doctrine of the 'Buddha-mind' which is to be realized in oneself.

D.: Bhagavan has said that without the grace of the Guru one cannot attain to the Self. What precisely does he mean by this? What is this Guru?

B.: From the standpoint of the path of knowledge, it is the supreme state of the Self. It is different from the ego which you call yourself.

D.: Then, if it is the supreme state of my own self, in what sense does Bhagavan mean that I cannot reach it without the grace of the Guru?

B.: The ego is the individuality and is not the same as the Lord of all. When it approaches the Lord with sincere devotion, He graciously assumes name and form and takes it to Himself. Therefore they say that the Guru is none other than the Lord. He is a human embodiment of Divine Grace.

This would seem to mean, then, that the Guru is the Lord or the Self manifested outwardly in human form and that this outward manifestation is necessary. But the questioner, in the present instance, was not convinced of this, since he knew that Bhagavan himself had

had no human Guru and that there are other cases on record also, especially among the founders of religions. He therefore continued:

D.: But there are some who seem to have had no human Guru at all?

B.: True. In the case of certain great souls, God reveals Himself as the Light of the Light from within.[1]

It occasionally happened that some questioner would openly raise the objection that Bhagavan himself had not a Guru, and in such cases his reply would be that the Guru need not necessarily take human form.

'Some who knew his teaching at secondhand suggested that he did not hold it necessary to have a Guru and explained the lack of explicit initiation in that way, but he rejected this suggestion unequivocally. S. S. Cohen has recorded a conversation on this subject with Dilip Kumar Roy, the celebrated musician of Sri Aurobindashram:'

Dilip: Some people report Maharshi to deny the need of a Guru. Others say the reverse. What does Maharshi say?

B.: I have never said that there is no need for a Guru.

Dilip: Sri Aurobindo often refers to you as having had no Guru.

B.: That depends on what you call Guru. He need not necessarily be in human form. Dattatreya had twenty-four Gurus—the elements, etc. That means that any form in the world was his Guru. Guru is absolutely necessary. The Upanishads say that none but a Guru can take a man out of the jungle of mental and sense perceptions, so there must be a Guru.

Dilip: I mean a human Guru. The Maharshi didn't have one.

B.: I might have had at some time or other. And didn't I sing hymns to Arunachala? What is a Guru? Guru is God or the Self. First a man prays to God to fulfil his desires, then a time comes when he does not pray for the fulfilment of a desire but

[1] S.D.B., V

for God Himself. So God appears to him in some form or other, human or non-human, to guide him as a Guru in answer to his prayer.

'It was only when some visitor brought up the subject that Sri Bhagavan himself had not had a Guru that he explained that the Guru need not necessarily take on a human form, and it was understood that this referred to very rare cases.'[1]

I shall return to this question later, but wish immediately to consider the implication of the saying that God, Guru and Self are the same. In the ordinary sense of the word, a guru is one who has been invested with the right to initiate disciples and prescribe a spiritual discipline for them; and in this sense, a valid investiture is necessary to validate his actions as a guru, just as valid ordination is necessary to validate the religious rites performed by a priest. A mass said by a duly ordained priest would be valid, whereas one said by a man of greater moral integrity and intellectual power who was not an ordained priest would not; and in exactly the same way, the genuineness of a guru and validity of his initiation and discipline is normally dependent rather on his legitimate investiture as the successor to a line of gurus than on his own inherent attainments. Bhagavan was little interested in this interpretation of the word guru, but he did accept it when asked.

D.: Can one derive any benefit from repeating incantations picked up casually without being initiated into them?

B.: No. One must be initiated into them and authorized to use them.

'Bhagavan then illustrated this saying by the following story: A king once visited his minister at the latter's house. There he was told that the minister was busy with his incantations. The king accordingly waited for him, and when he was free to meet him, asked him what incantation it was. The minister told him that it was the *Gayatri*. The king then asked the minister to initiate him into the use of it, but the latter declared that he was unable to. Thereupon the king learnt it from someone else and

[1] R.M., p. 143

next time he met the minister he repeated it to him and asked him whether it was right. The minister replied that the incantation was right but that it was not right for him to say it. The king asked why; the minister called an attendant who was standing nearby and told him to arrest the king. The order was not obeyed. The minister repeated it and still it was not obeyed. The king then flew into a temper and ordered the attendant to arrest the minister, which he immediately did. The minister laughed and said that that was the explanation the king had asked for.

' "How?" the king asked.

' "Because the order was the same, and the executive was the same, but the authority was different. When I pronounced the order there was no effect, but when you did, the effect was immediate. It is the same with incantations." '[1]

Normally, however, when Bhagavan said 'Guru' he meant something far greater than this, something different not in degree but in kind; he meant Sad-Guru, or Gurudeva, and that too in its highest meaning as nothing less than one who has realized his identity with the Self and abides therein constantly.

D.: What are the distinctive characteristics of a Guru by which one can recognize him?

B.: The Guru is one who at all times abides in the profound depths of the Self. He never sees any difference between himself and others and is quite free from the idea that he is the Enlightened or the Liberated One, while those around him are in bondage or the darkness of ignorance. His self-possession can never be shaken under any circumstances and he is never perturbed.

D.: What is the essential nature of *upadesa* or spiritual instruction given by the Guru?

B.: The word *upadesa* literally means restoring an object to its proper place. The mind of the disciple, having become differentiated from its true and primal state of Pure Being, which is the Self and which is described in the scriptures as *Sat-chit-*

ananda (Being-Consciousness-Bliss), slips away therefrom and, assuming the form of thought, constantly pursues objects of sense-gratification. Therefore it is assailed by the vicissitudes of life and becomes weak and dispirited. *Upadesa* consists in the Guru restoring it to its primal state and preventing it from slipping away from the state of Pure Being, of absolute identity with the Self, or, in other words, the Being of the Guru.

The word can also be understood as meaning to present an apparently distant object to close view; that is to say, it consists in the Guru showing the disciple what he had considered as distant and different from himself to be immediate and identical with himself.

D.: If, as this implies, the real being of the Guru is identical with that of the disciple, why have the scriptures categorically declared that, however great powers one may attain, he cannot attain Self-realization without the grace of the Guru?

B.: It is true that the being of the Guru is identical with that of the disciple; however, it is very seldom that a person can realize his true Being, without the grace of the Guru.[1]

It is not really the bodily individual that is the Guru.

B.: What is your idea of a guru? You think of him in human shape as a body of certain dimensions, complexion, etc. A disciple, after Realization, once said to his Guru: 'I now realize that you dwelt in my innermost heart as the one Reality in all my countless births and have now come before me in human shape and lifted this veil of ignorance. What can I do for you in return for such a great benefit?' And the Guru replied: 'You need not do anything. It is enough if you remain as you are in your true state.' That is the truth about the Guru.[2]

Bhagavan often explained that the Divine Guide, the true Guru, is in one's heart as well as being manifested outwardly. While the outward Guru turns one's mind inwards, the inner Guru pulls from

[1] S.I., pp. 7–8   [2] D.D., II, p. 96

within. Even one's environment does not happen by accident. The Guru creates the conditions necessary for one's quest.

D.: What is the Grace of the Guru?

B.: The Guru is the Self. At some time a man grows dissatisfied with his life and, not content with what he has, seeks the satisfaction of his desires through prayer to God. His mind is gradually purified until he longs to know God, more to obtain His Grace than to satisfy worldly desires. Then God's grace begins to manifest. God takes the form of a Guru and appears to the devotee, teaches him the Truth and, moreover, purifies his mind by association with him. The devotee's mind thus gains strength and is then able to turn inward. By meditation it is further purified until it remains calm without the least ripple. That calm Expanse is the Self.

'The Guru is both outer and inner. From outside he gives a push to the mind to turn inward while from inside he pulls the mind towards the Self and helps in quieting it. That is the Grace of the Guru. There is no difference between God, Guru and Self.'

D.: In the Theosophical Society they meditate in order to seek masters to guide them.

B.: The master is within; meditation is meant to remove the ignorant idea that he is only external. If he were some stranger whom you awaited, he would be bound to disappear also. What would be the use of a transient being like that? But as long as you think you are separate or that you are the body, so long is the outer master also necessary and He will appear as if with a body. When the wrong identification of yourself with the body ceases, the master will be found to be none other than the Self.

D.: Will the Guru help us to know the Self through initiation, etc.?

B.: Does the Guru hold you by the hand and whisper in your ear? You may imagine him to be what you are yourself. Because you think you have a body, you think that he has also and that he will do something tangible to you. His work lies within, in the spiritual realm.

D.: How is the Guru found?

B.: God, Who is immanent, in His Grace takes pity on the loving devotee and manifests Himself according to the devotee's development. The devotee thinks that he is a man and expects a relationship as between two physical bodies. But the Guru, who is God or the Self incarnate, works from within, helps the man to see his mistakes and guides him in the right path until he realizes the Self within.

D.: What should the devotee do then?

B.: He has only to act according to the words of the master and work inwardly. The master is both 'within' and 'without', as he creates conditions to drive you inward and at the same time prepares the 'interior' to drag you to the Centre. Thus he gives a push from 'without' and exerts a pull from 'within' so that you may be fixed at the Centre.

'You think that the world can be conquered by your own efforts. When you are frustrated externally and are driven inwards you feel, 'Oh, there is a power higher than man.' The ego is a very powerful elephant which cannot be brought under control by any creature less powerful than a lion, which, in this instance, is no other than the Guru, whose very looks make the elephant-like ego tremble and die. You will know in due course that your glory lies where you cease to exist. In order to gain that state, you should surrender yourself. Then the master sees that you are in a fit state to receive guidance and He guides you.'[1]

What is the significance of saying that the Guru is the manifestation of God or Self? Bhagavan spoke always from the point of view of non-duality, and from this point of view the disciple is also. The only difference is that the Guru has realized it and the disciple has not.

B.: So long as you seek Self-realization, the Guru is necessary. Guru is the Self. Take Guru to be the real Self, and yourself to be the individual self. The disappearance of this sense of duality is

[1] M.G., I, p. 35

the removal of ignorance. So long as duality persists in you, the Guru is necessary. Because you identify yourself with the body, you think the Guru too is the body. You are not the body, nor is the Guru. You are the Self and so is the Guru. This knowledge is gained by what you call Self-realization.[1]

'You mistake the body for the Guru. But the Guru himself does not make that mistake. He is the formless Self. That is within you. He appears outwardly only to guide you.'[2]

A curious paradox arises with the perfect Guru, the Self-realized man in constant, conscious identity with the Self. For the very reason that he is the complete and perfect Guru he will not call himself a Guru or call any his disciples, since that would be an affirmation of relationship and therefore of duality.

'Though he instructs his disciples, yet he does not call himself their Guru, realizing as he does that Guru and disciple are mere conventions born of *maya* (total illusion).'[3]

And indeed, Bhagavan initiated his disciples through silence, or in a dream when at a distance, or by look when they were in his bodily presence; but he did not call them his disciples or give the formal initiation that postulates duality. He watched over them constantly, prescribed a discipline for them verbally or guided them to it by the power of his silent grace. But he did not call himself their Guru.

D.: Isn't grace the gift of the guru?

B.: God, Grace and Guru are all synonymous and are both eternal and immanent. Isn't the Self already within? Is it for the Guru to bestow it by his look? If a Guru thinks so, he does not deserve that name. The books say there are many kinds of initiation. They also say that the Guru performs various rites with fire, water, incantations, etc., and call such fantastic performances initiation, as if the disciple became ripe only after such processes were gone through by the Guru.

[1] T., p. 282 [2] T., p. 499 [3] T., p. 449

'If the individual is sought, he is nowhere to be found. Such
is the Guru. Such is Dakshinamurthi. What did he do? He sat
silent. The disciples appeared before him. He maintained silence,
and their doubts were dispelled, which means they lost their
individual identities. *Jnana* (spiritual knowledge) is that silent
understanding and not the verbal definitions that are usually given
for it. Silence is the most potent form of work. However vast
and emphatic the scriptures may be, they fail in their effect. The
Guru is quiet and peace prevails in all. His silence is vaster and
more emphatic than all the scriptures put together. These
questions arise because of the feeling that, in spite of having been
here so long, heard so much, striven so hard, you have not gained
anything. The process that goes on inside you is not apparent to
you. In fact, the Guru is always within you.'[1]

Not all felt the grace, the power of silent initiation, immediately,
but Bhagavan reassured them.

D.: It is said that one look of a Mahatma is enough; that
idols, pilgrimages, etc., are not so effective; but I have been here
for three months and still do not know how I have been benefited
by the look of the Maharshi.

B.: The look has a purifying effect. Purification cannot be
visualized. Just as a piece of coal takes a long time to ignite and a
piece of charcoal a shorter time, while a heap of gunpowder is
ignited instantaneously, so it is with different types of men
coming in contact with a Mahatma.[2]

Incidentally, the devotee who raised this question stayed on and
became one of the staunchest and most devoted of all.

Complete faith in the Guru was necessary but, as explained in the
previous chapter, effort was also necessary.

D.: After leaving this Asramam in October, I was aware of
Bhagavan's peace enfolding me for about ten days. All the time,

[1] T., p. 398   [2] T., p. 155

while busy with work, there was an undercurrent of that peace of unity; it was almost like the dual consciousness while half asleep in a dull lecture. Then it faded out entirely and the old stupidities came instead.

'Work leaves no time for separate meditation. Is the constant reminder 'I am' and trying to feel this while actually at work enough?'

B.: It will become constant when the mind is strengthened. Repeated practice strengthens the mind, and such a mind is capable of holding on to the current. Then, whether you are engaged in work or not, the current remains unaffected and un-interrupted.[1]

It often happened that the disciple saw no improvement in himself despite the effort, but he was told to have faith in the Guru. The process might not be visible to himself and the improvement might be the greatest when least apparent.

'He evoked no spectacular changes in the devotees, for such changes may be a superstructure without foundation and collapse later. Indeed, it sometimes happened that a devotee would grow despondent, seeing no improvement at all in himself and would complain that he was not at all progressing. In such cases Bhagavan might offer consolation or might retort, "How do you know there is no progress?" And he would explain that it is the Guru, not the disciple, who sees the progress made; it is for the disciple to carry on perseveringly with his work even though the structure being raised may be out of sight of the mind.'[2]

There were some who desired a definite statement that Bhagavan was a Guru, but this he would not make.

'Mr. Evans-Wentz, the well-known writer on Tibetan Yoga, asked whether Bhagavan initiated disciples, but Bhagavan sat silent, giving no reply.

[1] T., p. 310 [2] R.M., p. 165

'Then one of the devotees took it on himself to answer that the Maharshi does not regard any as being outside himself and therefore none can be disciples to him. His grace is all-pervading and is bestowed in silence on any deserving individual.'[1]

Bhagavan heard this explanation and did not reject it. Sometimes he would explain that the guru-disciple relationship was necessary from the point of view of the disciple, since the latter viewed things from the standpoint of duality; and therefore the disciple could affirm that so and so was his Guru, although the Guru would not affirm that the other was his disciple.

D.: Bhagavan says he has no disciples?

B.: Yes.

D.: He also says that a Guru is necessary if one wishes to attain liberation.

B.: Yes.

D.: What then must I do? Has my sitting here all these years been just a waste of time? Must I go and look for some guru in order to receive initiation, seeing that Bhagavan says he is not a Guru?

B.: What do you think brought you here such a long distance and made you remain here so long? Why do you doubt? If there had been any need to seek a Guru elsewhere, you would have gone away long ago. The Guru or *Jnani* (Enlightened One) sees no difference between himself and others. For him all are *Jnanis*, all are one with himself, so how can a *Jnani* say that such and such is his disciple? But the unliberated one sees all as multiple, he sees all as different from himself, so to him the Guru-disciple relationship is a reality. For him there are three ways of initiation, by touch, look and silence. (Sri Bhagavan here gave the disciple to understand that his way was by silence, as he has to many on other occasions.)

D.: Then Bhagavan does have disciples?

B.: As I said, from Bhagavan's point of view there are no

disciples, but from that of the disciple, the Grace of the Guru is like an ocean. If he comes with a cup he will get only a cupful. It is no use complaining of the niggardliness of the ocean; the bigger the vessel the more he will be able to carry. It is entirely up to him.[1]

When the devotee pressed him once more for a confirmation he turned to the attendant and said humorously, 'Let him get a document from the sub-registrar and take it to the office and get the office stamp on it.'

In the following conversation, he implied clearly enough that he was to be regarded as the visible Guru.

D.: Can Sri Bhagavan help us to realize the Truth?

B.: Help is always there.

D.: Then, there is no need to ask questions. I do not feel the ever-present help.

B.: Surrender and you will find it.

D.: I am always at your feet. Will Bhagavan give us some *upadesa* to follow? Otherwise how can I get the help, living six hundred miles away?

B.: The Sad-Guru is within.

D.: The Sad-Guru is necessary to guide me to understand that fact.

B.: The Sad-Guru is within you.

D.: I want a visible Guru.

B.: That visible Guru says that he is within.

It was in keeping with the purely spiritual nature of Bhagavan's initiation and guidance that he was averse to touching his disciples or being touched by them. In the further part of the talk just quoted, the devotee requests:

D.: Will the Sad-Guru place his hand on my head to assure me of his help? Then I shall have the consolation of knowing that his promise will be fulfilled.

[1] R.M., p. 141

In such cases Bhagavan was apt either to remain silent or to turn it into a joke. On this occasion he took the latter course.

B.: Next you will be asking me for a bond and filing a suit if you imagine that the help is not forthcoming.[1]

It may be said by some readers of this book that this doctrine of God manifested as Guru was all right for those who had the good fortune to meet Bhagavan in his lifetime, but what of those who seek a Guru now? There are Gurus to be found, although the appearance on earth of a perfect Sad-Guru such as Bhagavan Ramana Maharshi, a *Jivanmukta* living in constant conscious identity with the Self, is a very rare thing.

D.: How can one know whether a particular person is competent to be a Guru?

B.: By the peace of mind you feel in his presence and by the respect you feel for him.

D.: And if it turns out that he is not competent, what will be the fate of the disciple who has implicit faith in him?

B.: The fate of each one will be according to his merit.[2]

But if the Guru has not attained the Supreme State, can he be regarded as a manifestation of God or the Self? In a way, he can. The disciple himself is the Self, although ignorant of his true identity. The entire outer world manifests tendencies and possibilities in himself and among these the person who functions as guru for him manifests the possibility of divine guidance, even without full awareness.

There is however another possibility also, and that is continued guidance by Bhagavan. It will be recalled that Bhagavan confirmed that the Guru need not necessarily take human form. He sometimes added that this happened only in rare cases. He himself had no human Guru. Just as, with Self-enquiry, he created a new path suitable to the conditions of the modern world, a path that can be followed without any outward forms, invisibly, while conforming to the outer conditions of modern life, so also he brought to men the possibility of silent, formless initiation, requiring no physical Guru. In his life-time

[1] T., p. 434   [2] T., p. 282

initiation was by look or silence. He often confirmed that the truest *upadesa* or spiritual instruction was by silence.

'The highest form of grace is silence. It is also the highest spiritual instruction. . . . All other modes of instruction are derived from silence and are therefore secondary. Silence is the primary form. If the Guru is silent the seeker's mind gets purified by itself.'[1]

The disciples of Bhagavan have found that the silent instruction continues as before. Others who have never met him in his lifetime have been drawn to him and begun to follow the guidance. If this seems strange to anyone, it means that he has not understood what Bhagavan was in his lifetime, that he identifies the Guru with the body. It is sometimes asked how a *Jivanmukta* continues to guide disciples after death, when he has merged in the Absolute, the Self of all. But the *Jivanmukta* is already consciously one with the Absolute, the Self of all, while still embodied. If this is not incompatible with initiation and guidance while he wears a body it is not afterwards. Death makes no difference to him, no change in his state. There is nothing more to be acquired, because He is that now; there is nothing to be lost, because he has already completely surrendered the ego.

'P. Bannerjee asked Bhagavan what is the difference between *Jivanmukti* (Realization while in the body) and *Videhamukti* (Realization after death).'

B.: There is no difference. For those who ask, it is said: A *Jnani* with a body is a *Jivanmukta* and he attains *videhamukti* when he sheds the body. But this difference exists only for the onlooker, not for the *Jnani*. His state is the same before and after the body is dropped. We think of the *Jnani* as a human form or as being in that form; but he knows that he is the Self, the one reality which is both inside and out, and which is not bounded by any form or shape. There is a verse in the Bhagavata (here Bhagavan quoted the verse in Tamil) which says: 'Just as a man who is drunk is not conscious whether his upper cloth is on his

[1] T., p. 518

body or has slipped away from it, the *Jnani* is hardly conscious of his body, and it makes no difference to him whether the body remains or has dropped off.'[1]

He did not encourage curiosity and seldom answered questions about the state of the *Jnani* or the Realized Man, but when asked whether the *Jnani* continues to perform a function after the death of the body, I have heard him reply briefly that in some cases he may. Also he himself confirmed, what his disciples know now from experience, that the Guru may continue to give guidance after the death of the body, when no longer in human form.

'Dr. Masalavala, retired Chief Medical Officer of Bhopal, who has been here for over a month and is in temporary charge of the Asramam hospital in the absence of Dr. K. Shiva Rao, put the following questions to Bhagavan and received the following answers:'

D.: Bhagavan says: 'The influence of the *Jnani* steals into the devotee in silence.' Bhagavan also says: 'Contact with great men, exalted souls, is one efficacious means of realizing one's true being.'
B.: Yes. What is the contradiction? *Jnani*, great men, exalted souls—does he differentiate between them?

'Thereupon I said "no" '.

B.: Contact with them is good. They will work through silence. By speaking their power is reduced. Speech is always less powerful than silence. So, silent contact is the best.
D.: Does the contact continue even after the dissolution of the physical body of the *Jnani* or only so long as he is in flesh and blood?
B.: The Guru is not the physical form. So contact will remain even after his physical form vanishes.[2]

[1] D.D., II, p. 109   [2] D.D., II, p. 181

He declared that one who has obtained the grace of the Guru would never be abandoned.

'He who has earned the grace of the Guru will undoubtedly be saved and never forsaken, just as the prey that has fallen into the tiger's jaw will never be allowed to escape.'[1]

Remembering this, perhaps, some devotees complained, when the death of his body was imminent, that he was abandoning them and asked what they could do without his continued guidance. He answered briefly:

'You attach too much importance to the body.'[2]

The implication was clear. The Guru is the same whether he wears a body or not. And his devotees have since found it so.

Having dealt with the need to pass from theory to practice, the possibility of practising in the conditions of the modern world without any outer observances, and the necessity for a Guru, the next two chapters will deal with the forms of practice that Bhagavan prescribed. His prescribing them openly is in itself remarkable. In their public writings and utterances the spiritual masters of all religions have dealt mainly with theory and said little or nothing about the practical discipline they enjoined. The reason for this is obvious. It is that, as Bhagavan explains in the story of the king and his minister quoted earlier in this chapter, a technique of spiritual training can be legitimately used and be effective for good only when the use of it has been authorized by one duly qualified. And yet Bhagavan himself openly expounded the methods he enjoined, both in speech and writing. Most of the books on which the present exposition is based were written and published during his lifetime, and he always showed interest in them and often recommended a questioner to turn to one of them for his answer. Even when it became clear that the life of his body was approaching its end he continued to show interest in their editing and publication. Why did he permit this, when he was insistent that no technique is valid without the authorization of the Guru? The only answer is that given above. Physical death made no difference. If the

[1] W., p. 44 [2] R.M., p. 185

Mukta can be a Guru before death, he can also after death. He becomes no more a *Mukta* by dying. The path that had been made open by his Grace to those who turn to him was not for his lifetime only or for those few only who could approach him physically. He said:

'They say that I am dying, but I am not going away. Where could I go? I am here.'[1]

[1] R.M., p. 185

5

SELF-ENQUIRY

Although refraining, for the reason given in the previous chapter, from describing himself as a Guru, Sri Bhagavan did in fact constantly act as such. When any visitor came with questions, he would turn the trend of them from theory to practice; and in explaining and enjoining methods of spiritual training he was as forthcoming as he was reluctant to expound mere theory. He often said that the true teaching was in silence; but this did not mean that verbal expositions also were not given. They indicated to the seeker in what way he should make an effort, while the silent influence on his heart helped him to do so.

As will be shown in the next chapter, Sri Bhagavan authorized many different methods; however, he laid the greatest emphasis on Self-enquiry and constantly recommended it, and therefore this method will be dealt with first.

It is not a new method. Indeed, being the most direct method of all, it must be the most ancient. However, in ancient times it had been a path reserved for the heroic few who could strive in solitude, withdrawn from the world in constant meditation. In recent times, as might be expected, it had become increasingly rare. What Bhagavan did was to restore it in a new form combined with *karma marga*, in such a way that it could be used in the conditions of the modern world. Since it requires no ritual or outer form, it is in fact the ideal method for the needs of our times. And yet it is not weakened or diluted by being adapted to modern conditions of life but remains central and direct.

'For the subsidence of the mind there is no other means more effective than Self-enquiry. Even though the mind subsides by other means, that is only apparently so, it will rise again.[1]

[1] W., p. 42

'This is the direct method. All other methods are practised while retaining the ego and therefore many doubts arise and the ultimate question still remains to be tackled in the end. But in this method the final question is the only one and is raised from the very beginning.[1]

'Self-enquiry leads directly to Self-realization by removing the obstacles which make you think that the Self is not already realized.[2]

'Meditation requires an object to meditate on, whereas in Self-enquiry there is only the subject and no object. That is the difference between them.[3]

D.: Why should Self-enquiry alone be considered the direct path to Realization?

B.: Because every kind of path except Self-enquiry presupposes the retention of the mind as the instrument for following it, and cannot be followed without the mind. The ego may take different and more subtle forms at different stages of one's practice but it is never destroyed. The attempt to destroy the ego or the mind by methods other than Self-enquiry is like a thief turning policeman to catch the thief that is himself. Self-enquiry alone can reveal the truth that neither the ego nor the mind really exists and enable one to realize the pure, undifferentiated Being of the Self or the Absolute.[4]

This statement that by the method of Self-enquiry the mind is not used was not always understood, and therefore Bhagavan, when asked, explained that it means that the mind is not taken for granted as a real entity but its very existence is questioned, and that this is the easiest way to dispel the illusion of its existence.

B.: To ask the mind to kill the mind is like making the thief the policeman. He will go with you and pretend to catch the thief, but nothing will be gained. So, you must turn inward and see where the mind rises from and then it will cease to exist. (In

[1] T., p. 146   [2] T., p. 298   [3] T., p. 390   [4] M.G., p. 48

reference to this answer, Sri Thambi Thorai of Jaffna, who has been living as a sadhu in Pelakothu for over a year, asked me whether asking the mind to turn inward and seek its source is not also employing the mind. I put this doubt before Bhagavan.)

B.: Of course we are employing the mind. It is well known and admitted that only with the help of the mind can the mind be killed. But instead of setting about saying there is a mind and I want to kill it, you begin to seek its source and you find it does not exist at all. The mind turned outwards results in thoughts and objects. Turned inwards it becomes itself the Self.[1]

It can be said that the mind ceases to exist or that it becomes transformed into the Self; the meaning is really the same. It does not mean that a person becomes mindless, like a stone, but that the Pure Consciousness of the Self is no longer confined within the narrow limits of an individualized mind and no longer sees through a glass darkly but with clarity and radiant vision.

'By steady and continuous investigation into the nature of the mind, the mind is transformed into That to which "I" refers; and that is in fact the Self. The mind has necessarily to depend for its existence on something gross; it never subsists by itself. It is the mind that is otherwise called the subtle body, ego, *jiva* or soul.

'That which arises in the physical body as "I" is the mind. If one enquires whence the "I" thought in the body arises in the first instance, it will be found that it is from *hrdayam* or the Heart. That is the source and stay of the mind. Or again, even if one merely continuously repeats to oneself inwardly "I-I" with the entire mind fixed thereon, that also leads to the same source.

'The first and foremost of all thoughts that arise in the mind is the primal "I" thought. It is only after the rise or origin of the "I" thought that innumerable other thoughts arise. In other words, only after the first personal pronoun, "I", has arisen, do the second and third personal pronouns (you, he, etc.) occur to the mind; and they cannot subsist without it.

[1] D.D., II, p. 40

'Since every other thought can occur only after the rise of the "I" thought, and since the mind is nothing but a bundle of thoughts, it is only through the enquiry: "Who am I?" that the mind subsides. Moreover, the integral "I" thought implicit in such enquiry, having destroyed all other thoughts, itself finally gets destroyed or consumed, just as a stick used for stirring the burning funeral pyre gets consumed.'[1]

It must already be apparent from these indications that Self-enquiry as taught by Bhagavan is something very different from the introversion of psychologists. In fact, it is not really a mental process at all. Introversion means studying the composition and contents of the mind, whereas this is an attempt to probe behind the mind to the Self from which it arises.

'When the mind or ego has to be discarded in any case, why waste time analysing it?

'To enquire: "Who am I that am in bondage?" and thus know one's real nature is the only Liberation. To keep the mind constantly turned inwards and to abide thus in the Self is the only Self-enquiry. Just as it is futile to examine the rubbish that has to be swept up only to be thrown away, so it is futile for him who seeks to know the Self to set to work enumerating the *tattvas* that envelop the Self and examining them instead of casting them away. He should consider the phenomenal world, with reference to himself, as merely a dream.'[2]

Similarly Self-enquiry differs fundamentally from psycho-analysis or any other kind of psychiatric treatment. Such treatment can only aim at producing a normal, healthy, integrated human being but not at transcending the bounds of the individual human state, since those who conduct it have themselves not done this and cannot open a road they have not trod. One thing, however, that Self-enquiry in its initial stages has in common with psychiatric treatment is that it serves to bring up hidden thoughts and impurities from the depths of the mind.

[1] W., p. 41   [2] W., p. 46

D.: Other thoughts arise more forcibly when one attempts meditation.

B.: Yes, all kinds of thoughts arise in meditation. That is only right; for what lies hidden in you is brought out. Unless it rises up, how can it be destroyed?

'Thoughts rise up spontaneously but only to be extinguished in due course, thus strengthening the mind.'[1]

D.: When I concentrate, all sorts of thoughts arise and disturb me. The more I try, the more thoughts rise up. What should I do?

B.: Yes, that will happen. All that is inside will try to come out. There is no other way except to pull the mind up each time it wants to go astray and fix it on the Self.[2]

D.: Bhagavan has often said that one must reject other thoughts when one begins the quest, but the thoughts are endless. If one thought is rejected another comes up and there seems to be no end at all.

B.: I do not say that you must keep on rejecting thoughts. If you cling to yourself, to the 'I' thought, and your interest keeps you to that single thought, other thoughts will get rejected and will automatically vanish.[3]

Just as Self-enquiry is not introspection as understood by the psychologists, so also it is not argument or speculation as understood by the philosophers.

D.: When I think, 'Who am I?', the answer comes: I am not this mortal body but am Consciousness or Self. And then another thought suddenly arises: Why has the Self entered manifestation? In other words, 'why has God created the world?'

B.: The enquiry: 'Who am I?' really means trying to find the source of the ego or of the 'I' thought. You are not to occupy the mind with other thoughts, such as 'I am not the body'. Seeking the source of the 'I' serves as a means of getting rid of all other thoughts. You should not allow any scope for other

[1] M.G., I, p. 19 [2] D.D., II, p. 44 [3] S.D.B., IV

thoughts such as you mention, but should keep the attention fixed on finding the source of the 'I' thought by asking, when any other thought arises, to whom it occurs; and if the answer is 'to me', you then resume the thought: 'Who is this "I" and what is its source?'[1]

Bhagavan did sometimes allow or even use mental argument but that was to convince the beginner of the unreality of the individual self or ego and thus induce him to take up Self-enquiry. The argument itself was not Self-enquiry.

D.: Who am I? How is the answer to be found?

B.: Ask yourself the question. The body (*annamayakosa*) and its functions are not 'I'. Going deeper, the mind (*manomayakosa*) and its functions are not 'I'. The next step takes one to the question: Wherefrom do these thoughts arise? The thoughts may be spontaneous, superficial, or analytical. They operate in the mind. Then who is aware of them? The existence of thoughts, their clear conception and operation, become evident to the individual. This analysis leads to the conclusion that the individuality is operative as the cognizer of the existence of thoughts and their sequence. This individuality is the ego, or, as people say, 'I'. *Vijnanamayakosa* (intellect) is only the sheath of the 'I' and not the 'I' itself. Enquiring further, the questions arise: Who is this 'I'? Wherefrom does it come? 'I' was not aware in sleep. Simultaneously with its rise, sleep changes to dream and wakefulness. But I am not concerned with the dream state just now. Who am I now, in the wakeful state? If I originated on waking from sleep, then the 'I' was covered up with ignorance. Such an ignorant 'I' cannot be what the scriptures refer to or the wise affirm. 'I' am beyond even sleep; 'I' must be here and now, and must be what I was all along in sleep and dream also, unaffected by the qualities of these states. 'I' must therefore be the unqualified substratum underlying these three states (after *anandamayakosa* is transcended).[2]

[1] D.D., II, p. 87   [2] T., p. 25

'Two Parsi ladies arrived from Ahmedabad and spoke with Bhagavan.'

L.: Bhagavan, we have been spiritually inclined from child-hood. We have read several books on philosophy and are attracted by Vedanta. So we read the Upanishads, Yoga Vasishta, Bhagavad Gita, etc. We try to meditate, but there is no progress in our meditation. We do not understand how to realize. Can you kindly help us towards realization?

B.: How do you meditate?

L.: I begin with asking myself 'Who am I?' and eliminate the body as not 'I', the breath as not 'I', the mind as not 'I', but then I am unable to proceed further.

B.: Well, that is all right so far as the mind goes. Your process is only mental. Actually all the scriptures mention this process only in order to guide the seeker to the Truth. The Truth cannot be directly indicated; that is why this mental process is used. You see, he who eliminates all the 'not-I' cannot eliminate the 'I'. In order to be able to say 'I am not this' or 'I am That', there must be the 'I' to say it. This 'I' is only the ego, or the 'I'-thought. After the rising up of this 'I'-thought, all other thoughts arise. The 'I'-thought is therefore the root thought. If the root is pulled out, all the rest is at the same time uprooted. Therefore seek the root 'I'; question yourself: 'Who am I?'; find out the source of the 'I'. Then all these problems will vanish and the pure Self alone will remain.

L.: But how am I to do it?

B.: The 'I' is always there, whether in deep sleep, in dream or in the waking state. The one who sleeps is the same as the one who is now speaking. There is always the feeling of 'I'. If it were not so you would have to deny your existence. But you do not. You say: 'I am'. Find out who is.

L.: I still do not understand. You say the 'I' is now the false 'I'. How am I to eliminate this wrong 'I'?

B.: You need not eliminate any false 'I'. How can 'I' eliminate itself? All that you need do is to find out its origin and stay there.

Your effort can extend only so far. Then the Beyond will take care of itself. You are helpless there. No effort can reach it.

L.: If 'I' am always—here and now—why do I not feel so?

B.: Who says that you do not? Does the real 'I' or the false 'I'? Ask yourself and you will find that it is the false 'I'. The false 'I' is the obstruction which has to be removed in order that the true 'I' may cease to be hidden. The feeling that 'I have not realized' is the obstruction to realization. In fact, it is already realized. There is nothing more to be realized. If there were, the realization would be something new which did not yet exist, but was to come about in the future; but whatever is born will also die. If realization is not eternal it is not worth having. Therefore, what we seek is not something that must begin to exist but only what is eternal but is veiled from us by obstructions. All that we need do is to remove the obstruction. What is eternal is not recognized as such owing to ignorance. Ignorance is the obstruction. Get rid of it and all will be well. This ignorance is identical with the 'I' thought. Seek its source and it will vanish.

'The "I"-thought is like a spirit which, although not palpable, rises up simultaneously with the body, flourishes with it and disappears with it. The body-consciousness is the wrong "I". Give it up. You can do so by seeking the source of "I". The body does not say: "I am". It is you who say "I am the body". Find out who this "I" is. Seek its source and it will vanish.'

L.: Then, will there be bliss?

B.: Bliss is co-eval with Being-Consciousness. All the arguments relating to the eternal Being apply to eternal Bliss also. Your nature is Bliss. Ignorance is now hiding the Bliss, but you have only to remove the ignorance for the Bliss to be freed.

L.: Should we not find out the ultimate reality of the world as individual and God?

B.: These are conceptions of the 'I'. They arise only after the advent of the 'I'-thought. Did you think of them in deep sleep? Yet you existed in sleep, and the same 'you' is speaking now. If they were real, would they not exist in your sleep also? They are dependent on the 'I' thought. Again, does the world tell you: 'I am the world'? Does the body say: 'I am the body'? You say: 'This is the world', 'this is the body', and so on. So these are only your conceptions. Find out who you are, and there will be an end of all doubts.

L.: What becomes of the body after realization? Does it continue to exist or not? We see realized people performing actions like other people.

B.: This question need not worry you now. You can ask it after realization if you feel like it. As for the realized beings, let them take care of themselves. Why do you worry about them? In fact, after realization, neither the body nor anything else will appear different from the Self.

L.: If we are always Being-Consciousness-Bliss, why does God place us in difficulties? Why did He create us?

B.: Does God come and tell you that He placed you in difficulties? It is you who say so. It is again the false 'I'. If that disappears, there will be no one to say that God created this or that. That which is does not even say 'I am'. For does any doubt arise that 'I am not'? Only if a doubt arose whether one was not a cow or a buffalo would one have to remind oneself that one is not but is a man; but this never happens. It is the same with one's own existence and realization.[1]

This last quotation brings us back from what Self-enquiry is not to what it is.

'When the mind unceasingly investigates its own nature, it transpires that there is no such thing as mind. This is the direct path for all.

'The mind is merely thoughts. Of all thoughts, the thought "I" is the root. Therefore, the mind is only the thought "I". Whence does this thought "I" arise? Seek for it within; it then vanishes. This is the pursuit of Wisdom. Where the "I" vanished, there appears an "I-I" by itself. This is the Infinite (*Purnam*).[2]

[1] T., p. 197   [2] S.I., pp. 17-20

'If the ego is, everything else also is. If the ego is not, nothing else is. Indeed the ego is all. Therefore the enquiry as to what this ego is, is the only way of giving up everything.

'The state of non-emergence of "I" is the state of being THAT. Without questing for that state of non-emergence of "I" and attaining It, how can one accomplish one's own extinction, from which the "I" does not revive? Without that attainment, how is it possible to abide in one's true state, where one is That?

'Just as a man would dive in order to get something that had fallen into the water, so one should dive into oneself with a keen one-pointed mind, controlling speech and breath, and find the place whence the "I" originates. The only enquiry leading to Self-realization is seeking the source of the word "I". Meditation on "I am not this; I am that" may be an aid to enquiry but it cannot be the enquiry. If one enquires "Who am I?" within the mind, the individual "I" falls down abashed as soon as one reaches the Heart and immediately Reality manifests itself spontaneously as "I-I". Although it reveals itself as "I", it is not the ego but the perfect Being, the Absolute Self.'[1]

B.: The notions of bondage and liberation are merely modifications of the mind. They have no reality of their own, and therefore cannot function of their own accord. Since they are modifications of something else, there must be an entity (independent of them) as their common source and support. If, therefore, one investigates into that source in order to know of whom the bondage or liberation is predicated, one will find that they are predicated of 'me', that is, oneself. If one then earnestly enquires 'Who am I?' one will see that there is no such thing as 'I' or 'me'. That which remains on seeing that the 'I' does not exist is realized vividly and unmistakably as self-luminous and subsisting merely as Itself. This vivid Realization, as a direct and immediate experience of the supreme Truth, comes quite naturally, with nothing uncommon about it, to everyone who,

[1] F.V., pp. 74–5

remaining just as he is, enquires introspectively without allowing the mind even for a moment to become externalized or wasting time in mere talk. There is, therefore, not the least doubt regarding the well-established conclusion that to those who have attained this Realization, and thus abide absolutely identical with the Self, there is neither bondage nor liberation.[1]

B.: The Self is Pure Consciousness. Yet a man identifies himself with the body which is insentient and does not itself say: 'I am the body'. Some one else says so. The unlimited Self does not. Who does? A spurious 'I' arises between Pure Consciousness and the insentient body and imagines itself to be limited to the body. Seek this and it will vanish like a phantom. The phantom is the ego or mind or individuality. All the *sastras* are based on the rise of this phantom, whose elimination is their purpose. The present state is mere illusion. Its dissolution is the goal and nothing else.[2]

Bhagavan here refers to the ego as the 'phantom' or a 'spurious I'. In the explanation to the two Parsi ladies quoted earlier, he spoke of a 'false I' and a 'true I'. For practical purposes, he did sometimes speak of giving up the false I in quest of the true, but that should not be taken as implying that there are two selves in a man. What he really meant was simply giving up the false identification of the 'I' as an individual being in order to realize its true identity as the universal Self. He frequently insisted that there are not two 'I's of which one can seek and know the other. According to the truth of non-duality, to see the Self is to be the Self; otherwise, there would be the duality of a subject and object and the trinity of the seer, sight and seen.

D.: How is one to realize the Self?
B.: Whose Self? Find out.
D.: Mine; but, who am I?
B.: It is you who must find out.
D.: I don't know.
B.: Just think over the question. Who is it that says: 'I

[1] S.I., p. 33 [2] T., p.4 27

don't know'? Who is the 'I' in your statement? What is not known?

D.: Somebody or something in me.

B.: Who is that somebody? In whom?

D.: Perhaps some power.

B.: Find out.

D.: Why was I born?

B.: Who was born? The answer is the same to all your questions.

D.: Who am I then?

B. (smiling): Have you come to examine me? You must say who you are.

D.: However much I may try, I do not seem to catch the 'I'. It is not even clearly discernible.

B.: Who is it that says that the 'I' is not discernible? Are there two 'I's in you, that one is not discernible to the other?

D.: Instead of enquiring: 'Who am I?', can I put the question to myself: 'Who are you?', so that my mind may be fixed on you whom I consider to be God in the form of the Guru. Perhaps I would come nearer to the goal of my quest by that enquiry than by asking myself: 'Who am I?'.

B.: Whatever form your enquiry may take, you must finally come to the one 'I', the Self. All these distinctions made between 'I' and 'you', master and disciple, etc., are merely a sign of ignorance. The supreme 'I' alone is. To think otherwise is to delude oneself.

'Therefore, since your aim is to transcend here and now these superficialities of physical existence through self-enquiry, where is the scope for making the distinctions of "you" and "I" which pertain only to the body? When you turn the mind inwards, seeking the source of thought, where is the "you" and where the "I"? You should seek and be the Self that includes all.'

D.: But, isn't it funny that the 'I' should be searching for the 'I'? Doesn't the enquiry, 'Who am I?' turn out in the end to be an empty formula? Or am I to put the question to myself endlessly, repeating it like some *mantra*?

B.: Self-enquiry is certainly not an empty formula; it is more than the repetition of any *mantra*. If the enquiry: 'Who am I?' were mere mental questioning, it would not be of much value. The very purpose of Self-enquiry is to focus the entire mind at its source. It is not, therefore, a case of one 'I' searching for another 'I'. Much less is Self-enquiry an empty formula, for it involves an intense activity of the entire mind to keep it steadily poised in pure Self-awareness. Self-enquiry is the one infallible means, the only direct one, to realize the unconditioned, absolute Being that you really are.[1]

The following passages show still more clearly that it is a question of tracing the 'I' thought back to its source, not of one 'I' discovering another.

V.: I am told that according to your school I must find out the source of my thought. How am I to do it?

B.: I have no school; however, it is true that one should trace the source of all thoughts.

V.: Suppose I have the thought 'horse', and try to trace its source. I find that it is due to memory and the memory in its turn is due to prior perception of the object 'horse', but that is all.

B.: Who asked you to think about all that? All those are also thoughts. What good will it do you to go on thinking about memory and perception? It will be endless, like the old dispute, which came first, the tree or the seed. Ask who has this perception and memory. That 'I' that has the perception and memory, whence does it arise? Find this out. Because perception or memory or any other experience only comes to that 'I'. You do not have such experiences during sleep and yet you say that you existed during sleep. And you exist now too. That shows that the 'I' continues while other things come and go.

V.: I am asked to find out the source of 'I' and in fact that is what I want to find out, but how can I? What is the source from which I came?

[1] M.G., II, p. 45

B.: You came from the same source in which you were during sleep. Only during sleep you could not know where you entered. That is why you must make the enquiry while awake.

'Some of us advised the visitor to read "Who am I?" and "Ramana Gita" and Bhagavan also told him he might do so. He did so during the day and in the evening he said to Bhagavan: "Those books prescribe Self-enquiry, but how is one to do it?"'

B.: That must also be prescribed in the books.

V.: Am I to concentrate on the thought: 'Who am I?'

B.: It means that you must concentrate to see where the 'I' thought arises. Instead of looking outwards, look inwards and see where the 'I' thought arises.

V.: And Bhagavan says that if I see that, I shall realize the Self?

B.: There is no such thing as realizing the Self. How is one to realize or make real what is real? People all realize or regard as real what is unreal, and all they have to do is to give up doing so. When you do that, you will remain as you always are and the Real will be Real. It is only to help people give up regarding the unreal as real that all the religions and practices taught by them have come into being.

V.: Whence comes birth?

B.: Whose birth?

V.: The Upanishads say: He who knows Brahman becomes Brahman.

B.: It is not a matter of becoming but of Being.[1]

'There is no such thing as realizing the Self'—Bhagavan has often said this in order to remind those who asked that the Self alone is, now and eternally, and is not something new to be discovered. This paradox is of the essence of non-dualism.

'In answer to a question as to what is the best way to the goal, Bhagavan said: "There is no goal to be reached. There is nothing

[1] D.D., I, p. 58

to be attained. You are the Self. You exist always. Nothing more can be predicted of the Self than that it exists. Seeing God or the Self is only being the Self, that is yourself. Seeing is Being. You, being the Self, want to know how to attain the Self. It is like a man being at Ramanasramam and asking how many ways there are of going to Ramanasramam and which is the best way for him. All that is required of you is to give up the thought that you are this body and give up all thoughts of external things or the non-Self. As often as the mind goes out towards objects, stop it and fix it in the Self or 'I'. That is all the effort required on your part.'' '[1]

Despite this paradox, however, Bhagavan also stressed the necessity of effort, as explained in Chapter 2 of this book.

'Ceaseless practice is essential until one attains without the least effort that natural and primal state of mind which is free from thought, in other words, until the "I", "my" and "mine" are completely eradicated and destroyed.'[2]

It is in order to safeguard the viewpoint that there is nothing new to be discovered that Advaita explains that it is only a question of removing the screen of ignorance, just as by removing water-plants one reveals beneath them the water that was already there, or as the removal of clouds reveals the blue sky that was there already but was hidden by them.

D.: How can one know the Self?
B.: The Self always is. There is no knowing it. It is not some new knowledge to be acquired. What is new and not here and now cannot be permanent. The Self always is, but knowledge of it is obstructed and the obstruction is called ignorance. Remove the ignorance and knowledge shines forth. In fact, it is not the Self that has this ignorance or even knowledge. They are only accretions to be cleared away. That is why the Self is said to be

[1] D.D., II, p. 291   [2] S.I, p. 21

beyond knowledge and ignorance. It remains as it naturally is—
that is all.[1]

This concentration on the Self, of course, requires intense control
of the mind and many complained that it was not easy.

'In the evening a visitor asked Bhagavan how to control the
wandering mind. He began by saying that it was a question
which particularly troubled him. Bhagavan replied, laughing:
"That is nothing particular to you. That is what everybody asks
and what is dealt with by all the scriptures, such as the Gita.
What other way is there except to draw the mind back every
time it strays or turns outwards, as advised in the Gita? Of course
it is not an easy thing to do. It will come only with practice."
'The visitor said that the mind strays after what it desires
and won't stay fixed on the object we set before it.'

When there was this sort of complaint, Bhagavan sometimes
answered that Self-enquiry does not set any object before the mind
but simply turns it on itself, seeking its source. On this occasion,
however, he answered from the point of view of desire or happiness.

'Everybody seeks only what brings him happiness. Your
mind wanders out after some object or other because you think
that happiness comes from it, but find out where all happiness
comes from, including that which you regard as coming from
sense objects. You will find that it all comes from the Self alone,
and then you will be able to abide in the Self.'[2]

Sometimes people complained of the difficulty of quelling thoughts.
Bhagavan brought them round again to Self-enquiry by reminding
them that it is the thinker or, in case of doubt, the doubter whom one
must examine. There may be a thousand doubts but one does not
doubt the existence of the doubter. Who is he?

'All doubts will cease only when the doubter and his source

[1] T., p. 49   [2] D.D., II, p. 253

have been found. It is no use endlessly removing doubts. If we clear up one another will arise and there will be no end to them. But if the doubter himself is found to be really non-existent by seeking his source then all doubts will cease.'[1]

Mind-control, of course, means concentration; but by concentration Bhagavan did not mean concentrating on one thought (although he did not always discourage this) but concentrating on the sense of being, the feeling of 'I am', and excluding all thoughts.

B.: Concentration is not thinking of one thing. On the contrary, it is excluding all thoughts, since all thoughts obstruct the sense of one's true being. All efforts are to be directed simply to removing the veil of ignorance.[2]

In a number of passages already quoted, Bhagavan does not only tell the questioner to investigate the 'I' thought but to find out where it arises. This connects Self-enquiry with concentration on the heart at the right side (referred to in Chapter 1) and shows still more clearly that it is not a mental process. Indeed, an actual vibration that can be felt physically arises in this centre during Self-enquiry.

'Concentrating the mind solely on the Self will lead to happiness or bliss. Drawing in the thoughts, restraining them and preventing them from straying outwards is called detachment (*vairagya*). Fixing them in the Self is spiritual practice (*sadhana*). Concentrating on the heart is the same as concentrating on the Self. Heart is another name for Self.'[3]

G. V. Subbaramaiah: Is it stated in any books that for ultimate and final realization one must ultimately come to the Heart, even after reaching *Sahasrara* (the thousand-petalled lotus, the centre in the crown of the head) and that the Heart is at the right side?

B.: No, I have not come across this in any book, although in a Malayalam book on medicine I came across a stanza locating

[1] D.D., II, p. 28   [2] T., p. 398   [3] D.D., II, p. 249

the heart on the right side and I have translated it into Tamil in the Supplement to the 'Forty Verses'.

'We know nothing about the other centres. We cannot be sure what we arrive at on concentrating on them and realizing them. But as the "I" arises from the heart it must sink back and merge there for Self-realization. Anyway, that has been my experience.[1]

'Know that the pure and changeless Self-awareness in the Heart is the Knowledge which, through destruction of the ego, bestows Liberation.

'The body is inert like an earthen pot. Since it has no I-consciousness and since in deep sleep, when bodiless, we experience our natural being, the body cannot be the I. Who then is it that causes I-ness? Whence is he? In the Heart-cave of those who thus enquire and who know and abide as the Self, Lord Arunachala Siva shines forth as Himself as the "That-am-I" Consciousness.'[2]

D.: Bhagavan was saying that the heart is the centre of the Self?

B.: Yes, it is the one supreme centre of the Self. You need have no doubts about that. The real Self is there in the heart behind the ego-self.

D.: Will Bhagavan please tell me where in the body it is?

B.: You cannot know it with your mind or picture it with your imagination, although I tell you that it is here (pointing to the right side of the chest). The only direct way to realize it is to stop imagining and try to be yourself. Then you automatically feel that the centre is there. It is the centre spoken of in the scriptures as the heart-cavity.

D.: Can I be sure that the ancients meant this centre by the term 'heart'?

B.: Yes, you can, but you should try to have the experience rather than locate it. A man does not have to go and find where his eyes are in order to see. The heart is there, always open to

[1] D.D., I, p. 41   [2] F.V.S., p. 78

you, if you care to enter it, always supporting your movements, although you may be unaware of it. It is perhaps more correct to say that the Self is the Heart. Really the Self is the centre and is everywhere aware of itself as the Heart or Self-awareness. . . .

D.: When Bhagavan says that the Heart is the supreme centre of the Spirit or the Self, does that imply that it is not one of the six yogic centres (*chakras*)?

B.: The yogic centres, counting from the bottom upwards, are a series of centres in the nervous system. They represent various stages, each having its own kind of power or knowledge, leading to the *Sahasrara,* the thousand-petalled lotus in the brain, where is seated the Supreme *Shakti* (power). But the Self that supports the whole movement of the *Shakti* is not located there but supports it from the heart-centre.

D.: Then it is different from the manifestation of *Shakti?*

B.: Really there is no manifestation of *Shakti* apart from the Self. The Self became all these *shaktis.* When the yogi attains the highest state of spiritual awareness (*samadhi*) it is the Self in the Heart that supports him in that state whether he is aware of it or not. But if his awareness is centred in the heart, he realizes that, whatever centres or states he may be in, he is always the same truth, the same heart, the one Self, the spirit that is present throughout, eternal and immutable. The Tantra Sastra calls the heart *Surya Mandala* or the solar orb, and the *Sahasrara Chandra Mandala* or lunar orb. This shows the relative importance of the two.[1]

Just as this concentration on the heart establishes a point of contact with yoga, so also Bhagavan sometimes pointed out the affinity with *bhakti,* the path of devotion, and said that the two paths lead to the same end. Perfect devotion means complete surrender of the ego to God or Guru conceived of as other than oneself, while Self-enquiry leads to dissolution of the ego. More will be said about *bhakti marga* in the next chapter, but the following explanation shows how the two paths converge.

[1] S.D.B., XVII

D.: If the 'I' is an illusion, who is it that casts off the illusion?

B.: The 'I' casts off the illusion of the 'I' and yet remains 'I'. This is the paradox of Self-realization. The Realized do not see any paradox in it. Consider the case of the worshipper. He approaches God and prays to be absorbed in Him. He then surrenders himself in faith and by concentration. And what remains afterwards? In the place of the original 'I' self-surrender leaves a residuum of God in which the 'I' is lost. That is the highest form of devotion or surrender and the peak of detachment.

'You may give up this and that of "my" possessions, but if, instead, you give up "I" and "mine" all is given up at a stroke and the very seed of possession is destroyed. Thus the evil is nipped in the bud or crushed in the germ. But detachment must be very strong to do this. The craving to do it must equal the craving of a man who is held under water to rise to the surface and breathe.'[1]

If distracting thoughts are a danger on one side, sleep is on the other. In fact, people who are beginning a spiritual path may find themselves assailed by an overpowering wave of sleepiness whenever they begin to meditate. And then, if they stop meditating, this passes and they are not sleepy at all. This is simply one form of the ego's resistance and has to be broken down.

'Mr. Bhargava also said something about sleep and this led Bhagavan to speak about sleep as follows:

'What is required is to remain fixed in the Self always. The obstacles to that are distraction by things of the world (including sense objects, desires and tendencies) on the one hand and sleep on the other. Sleep is always mentioned in the books as the first obstacle to *samadhi* and various methods are prescribed for overcoming it according to the stage of evolution of the person concerned. First, one is enjoined to give up all worldly distractions and to restrict sleep. But then it is said, for instance in the Gita,

[1] T., p. 28

that one need not give up sleep entirely. One should not sleep at all during daytime, and even during night restrict sleep to the middle portion, from about ten to two. But another method that is prescribed is not to bother about sleep at all. Whenever it overtakes you, you can do nothing about it, so simply remain fixed in the Self or in meditation every moment of your waking life and take up meditation again the moment you wake, and that will be enough. Then, even during sleep, the same current of thought or meditation will be working. This is evident because if a man goes to sleep with any strong thought working in his mind he finds the same thought when he wakes up. It is of the man who does this with meditation that it is said that even his sleep is *samadhi*.'[1]

It is important to remember this, because the Maharshi often spoke of sleep as an example of the egoless state. As the above passage shows, he did not mean that physical sleep is to be encouraged. That is only a dark, unconscious counterpart of the true egoless state, which is pure Consciousness.

Another source of questions among those who continued further with meditation was that they sometimes came up against a blank or void or a feeling of fear, but they were told to carry on, holding firmly to that which experiences the void or fear. The same answer was also given to those who experienced a state of bliss. There can be neither fear nor pleasure, neither vision nor void, without someone to experience it.

D.: When I reach the thoughtless stage in my *sadhana*, I enjoy a certain pleasure but sometimes I also experience a vague fear which I cannot properly describe.

B.: Whatever you experience, you should never rest content with it. Whether you feel pleasure or fear, ask yourself who feels it and continue your efforts until both pleasure and fear are transcended and all duality ceases and the Reality alone remains. There is nothing wrong in such things being experienced, but you must never stop at that. For instance you must never rest content with

[1] D.D., I, p. 73

the pleasure of *laya* experienced when thought is quelled but must press on until all duality ceases.[1]

'In the afternoon the following questions were put by Mr. Bhargava, an elderly visitor from Jhansi in U.P.: (1) How am I to search for the "I" from start to finish? (2) When I meditate, I reach a stage where there is a vacuum or void. How should I proceed from there?'

B.: Never mind whether there are visions or sounds or anything else or whether there is void. Are you present during all this or are you not? You must have been there during the void to be able to say that you experienced a void. To be fixed in that 'you' is the quest from start to finish. In all books on Vedanta you will find this question of a void or nothing being left raised by the disciple and answered by the Guru. It is the mind that sees objects and has experiences and that finds a void when it ceases to see and experience, but that is not 'you'. You are the constant illumination that lights up both the experience and the void. It is like the theatre light that enables you to see the theatre, the actors, and the play while the play is going on but also remains alight and enables you to say that there is no play on when it is all finished. Or there is another illustration. We see objects all around us but in complete darkness we do not see them and we say: 'I see nothing.' In the same way, you are there even in the void you mention.

'You are the witness of the three bodies: the gross, the subtle and the causal, and of the three times: past, present and future, and also this void. In the story of the tenth man, when each of them counted and thought they were only nine, each one forgetting to count himself, there is a stage when they think one is missing and do not know who it is; and that corresponds to the void. We are so accustomed to the notion that all that we see around us is permanent and that we are this body, that when all this ceases to exist we imagine and fear that we also have ceased to exist.

[1] D.D., I, p. 7

'Bhagavan also quoted verses 212 and 213 from Viveka Chuda-mani in which the disciple says: After I eliminate the five sheaths as not-Self, I find that nothing at all remains; and the Guru replies that the Self or That by which all modifications, including the ego and all its creatures and their absence (that is the void), are perceived, is always there.

'Bhagavan continued and said: "The nature of the Self or 'I' must be illumination. You perceive all modifications and their absence. How? To say that you get the illumination from another would raise the question how he got it and there would be no end to the chain of reasoning. So you yourself are the illumination. The usual illustration of this is the following. You make all kinds of sweets of various ingredients and in various shapes and they all taste sweet because there is sugar in all of them and sweetness is the nature of sugar. And in the same way all experiences and the absence of them contain the illumination which is the nature of the Self. Without the Self they cannot be experienced, just as without sugar no one of the articles you make can taste sweet." Later he continued: "First one sees the Self as objects, then one sees the Self as void, then one sees the Self as the Self; only in this last case there is no seeing because seeing is being."[1]

Before closing this chapter it may be well to give a few more specific rules or rather to indicate that they exist but are not essential. It is usual to conduct what is called 'meditation' during regular hours, morning and evening, sitting with a straight spine and closed eyes. I say 'what is called meditation' because this word is commonly used for Self-enquiry and concentration on the 'I am' or the heart, as described in this chapter. It is, of course, far from the mental reflection that commonly goes by that name. In India it is usual to sit cross-legged on the ground. However, all such rules of technique are less important in Self-enquiry than with other less direct methods. Indeed, this is obvious from the fact that Self-enquiry has gradually to be extended from set hours of meditation until it becomes the undercurrent of all thoughts and actions.

[1] D.D., I, p. 71

'Mr. Evans-Wentz asked a few questions. They related to yoga. He wanted to know if it was right to kill animals such as tigers, deer, etc., and use the skin as a seat for the yoga-posture (*asana*).'

B.: The mind is the tiger or the deer.

D.: If everything is illusion, can one then take life?

B.: Who has the illusion? That is what you must find out. In fact, everyone is a killer of the Self (*atmahan*) at every moment of his life.

D.: Which posture is the best?

B.: Any posture, possibly *sukhasana* (the easy or half-Buddha posture). But that is immaterial for *jnana* (the path of knowledge).

D.: Does posture indicate temperament?

B.: Yes.

D.: What are the properties and effects of a tiger's skin or wool or a deer's skin as a seat?

B.: Some people have found out and described them in books on yoga. They correspond to conductors and non-conductors of magnetism, etc. But all this is of no importance on the path of knowledge (*jnana marga*). Posture really means steadfastness in the Self and is inward.

D.: Which is the most suitable time for meditation?

B.: What is time?

D.: Tell me what it is.

B.: Time is only an idea. There is only Reality. Whatever you think it is, it appears to be. If you call it time, it is time. If you call it existence, it is existence, and so on. After calling it time, you divide it into days and nights, months, years, hours, minutes, etc. Time is immaterial for the path of knowledge. But some of these rules and disciplines are good for beginners.

D.: Does Bhagavan recommend any special posture for Europeans?

B.: It depends on the mental equipment of the individual. There are no hard and fast rules.

D.: Is meditation to be practised with eyes open or closed?

B.: It may be done either way. The important thing is that the mind should be turned inwards and kept active in its quest. Sometimes it happens that when the eyes are closed latent thoughts rush forth with great vigour; but, on the other hand, it may be difficult to turn the mind inwards with the eyes open. It requires strength of mind. The mind is pure by nature but contaminated by taking in objects. The great thing is to keep it active in its quest without taking in external impressions or thinking of other things.[1]

Although, as will be shown in the next chapter, the Maharshi approved of various methods and authorized them when they suited the practitioner, he was nevertheless careful that they should not be confused with the direct method of Self-enquiry. For instance, there are indirect paths which sedulously cultivate the various virtues; but when asked about this he replied simply that on the direct path of Self-enquiry no such technique is necessary.

D.: It is said in some books that one should cultivate all the good or divine qualities in order to prepare oneself for Self-realization.

B.: All good or divine qualities are included in spiritual knowledge and all bad or demonic qualities are included in ignorance. When knowledge comes, ignorance goes and all the divine qualities appear automatically. If a man is Self-realized he cannot tell a lie or commit a sin or do anything wrong. It is no doubt said in some books that one should cultivate one virtue after another and thus prepare for ultimate realization, but for those who follow the *jnana marga* (path of knowledge) Self-enquiry is quite enough for acquiring all the divine qualities; they need not do anything else.[2]

In general, he approved the use of incantations by those who found them helpful but he was insistent that Self-enquiry should not become one.

[1] T., p. 17   [2] D.D., I, p. 69

D.: Please tell me how I am to realize the Self? Am I to make an incantation of 'Who am I?'

B.: No. It is not intended to be used as an incantation.[1]

However the method which is most apt to be confused with Self-enquiry is the meditation 'I am He' and therefore he frequently warned against this confusion.

'Self-enquiry is a different method from the meditation "I am Siva" or "I am He". I rather lay stress on Self-knowledge, because you are first concerned with yourself before you proceed to know the world and its Lord. The "I am He" or "I am Brahman" meditation is more or less mental but the quest for the Self of which I speak is a direct method and is superior to the other. For as soon as you undertake the quest and begin to go deeper and deeper, the real Self is waiting there to receive you and then whatever is done is done by something else and you have no hand in it. In this process all doubts are automatically given up just as one who sleeps forgets all his cares for the time being.[2]

'Although the scriptures proclaim "Thou art That", it is only a sign of weakness to meditate "I am That, not this", because you are eternally That. What has to be done is to investigate what one really is and remain That.[3]

'Only if the thought "I am a body" occurs will the meditation "I am not this, I am that" help one to abide as that. Why should you for ever be thinking "I am That"? Is it necessary for a man to go on thinking "I am a man"? Are we not always That?[4]

'A Punjabi announced himself to the Maharshi as having been directed here by Sri Sankaracharya of Kama Koti Peeta from Jalesvar near Puri-Jagannath. He is a world-traveller. He has practised Hatha-Yoga and some contemplation along the lines of "I am Brahman". In a few moments blank prevails, his brain gets

---

[1] T., p. 486   [2] S.D.B., vii   [3] F.V., p. 75   [4] F.V., p. 76

heated and he becomes afraid of death. He wants guidance from the Maharshi.'

B.: Who sees the blank?

D.: I know that I see it.

B.: The Consciousness overlooking the blank is the Self.

D.: That doesn't satisfy me. I can't realize it.

B.: The fear of death arises only after the 'I' thought arises. Whose death do you fear? To whom does the fear come? So long as there is identification of the Self with the body there will be fear.

D.: But I am not aware of my body.

B.: Who says that he is not aware?

D.: I don't understand.

'He was then asked to say what exactly was his method of meditation. He said: *Aham Brahmasmi* (I am Brahman).

B.: 'I am Brahman' is only a thought. Who says it? Brahman himself does not say so. What need is there for him to say it? Nor can the real 'I' say so. For 'I' always abides as Brahman. So it is only a thought. Whose thought is it? All thoughts come from the unreal 'I', that is the 'I' thought. Remain without thinking. So long as there is thought there will be fear.

D.: When I go on thinking on this line, forgetfulness ensues. The brain becomes heated and I become afraid.

B.: Yes, the mind is concentrated in the brain and hence you get a hot sensation there. That is because of the 'I' thought. So long as there is thought there will be forgetfulness. There is the thought 'I am Brahman'; then forgetfulness supervenes; then the 'I' thought arises and simultaneously the fear of death also. Forgetfulness and thought exist only for the 'I' thought. Investigate this and it will disappear like a phantom. What remains then is the real I. That is the Self. The thought 'I am Brahman' may be an aid to concentration in so far as it keeps other thoughts away and persists alone. But then you have to ask whose thought it is. It will be found to come from the 'I'. But where does the 'I' thought come from? Probe into it and it will vanish. The Supreme Self will shine forth of itself. No further effort is needed. When the one real 'I' remains alone, it will not need to say 'I am Brahman'. Does a man go on repeating 'I am a man'? Unless he is challenged why should he declare himself a man? Does anyone mistake himself for an animal that he should say 'No, I am not an animal, I am a man'? Similarly, since Brahman or 'I' alone, is, there is no one to challenge it, and so there is no need to repeat 'I am Brahman.'[1]

Throughout this chapter, Self-enquiry has been spoken of mainly as a spiritual exercise or 'meditation' to be practised at certain fixed times. It does indeed begin so and, so long as effort is needed, such times of intensive meditation continue to be helpful, but that is not enough. The Self-awareness which begins to be experienced during such meditation has to be cultivated at other times also and indeed begins to awaken spontaneously, forming an undercurrent to one's activities. The aim is to make it more and more continuous. It will be seen that this explains Bhagavan's injunction, referred to in Chapter 3, to conduct one's spiritual quest in the world and not to retire to a hermitage.

D.: Is a set meditation necessary for strengthening the mind?
B.: Not if you keep the idea always before you, that it is not your work. At first effort is needed to remind yourself of it, but later on it becomes natural and continuous. The work will go on of its own accord and your peace will remain undisturbed. Meditation is your true nature. You call it meditation now, because there are other thoughts distracting you. When these thoughts are dispelled, you remain alone—that is, in the state of meditation free from thoughts; and that is your real nature, which you are now trying to realize by keeping away other thoughts. Such keeping away of other thoughts is now called meditation. But when the practice becomes firm, the real nature shows itself as true meditation.[2]

For the reason mentioned in the previous chapter, a guru often

[1] T., p. 202   [2] M.G., I, p. 19

withholds the technique of spiritual practice as a secret to be revealed only to those whom he finds fit and initiates into it personally. However, with Self-enquiry as taught by Bhagavan, no such precaution is necessary. It is a person's own understanding that opens this method to him, or his lack of understanding that closes it.

D.: May I be assured that there is nothing further to be learnt, so far as the technique of spiritual practice is concerned, than what is written in Bhagavan's books? I ask because in all other systems, the guru holds back some secret technique to reveal to his disciple at the time of initiation.

B.: There is nothing more to be known than what you find in the books. No secret technique. It is all an open secret in this system.[1]

---

[1] D.D., II, p. 284

6

OTHER METHODS

D.: Which method is the best?

B.: That depends on the temperament of the individual. Every person is born with the *samskaras* (characteristics or tendencies) from his past lives. One method will prove easy to one person and another to another. There can be no general rule.[1]

In the following passage, Bhagavan indicates the purpose of all the methods, the goal they aim at.

'There are many methods. You may practise Self-enquiry, asking yourself "Who am I?"; or if that does not appeal to you, you may meditate on "I am Brahman", or some other theme; or you may concentrate on an incantation or invocation. The object in every case is to make the mind one-pointed, to concentrate it on one thought and thereby exclude the many other thoughts. If we do this, the one thought also eventually goes and the mind is extinguished at its source.'[2]

'Dr. Masalawala placed in Bhagavan's hands a letter he had received from his friend V. K. Ajgaonkar, a gentleman of about 35 (a follower of Jnaneswar Maharaj), who is said to have attained *Jnana* in his 28th year. The letter said: "You call me *purna*. Who is not *purna* in this world?". Bhagavan agreed and continuing in the vein in which he discoursed this morning

[1] T., p. 580 [2] D.D., II, p. 30

(15-3-46), said: "We first limit ourselves and then seek to become unlimited as in fact we always are. All our effort is only directed to giving up the notion that we are limited. . . ."

'The letter went on to say: "Ramana Maharshi is an exponent of the Ajata doctrine of Advaita Vedanta. Of course it is a bit difficult." Bhagavan remarked on this: "Somebody has told him so. I do not teach only the Ajata doctrine. I approve of all schools. The same truth has to be expressed in different ways to suit the capacity of the hearer. The Ajata doctrine says: 'Nothing exists except the one Reality. There is no birth or death, no projection or drawing in, no *sadhaka*, no *mumukshu*, no *mukta*, no bondage, no liberation. The one unity alone exists for ever. To such as find it difficult to grasp this truth and who ask: "How can we ignore this solid world we see all around us?" the dream experience is pointed out and they are told, "All that you see depends upon the seer. Apart from the seer, there is no seen." This is called *drishtisrishti vada* or the argument that one first creates out of his mind and then sees what his mind has created. To such as cannot grasp even this and who further argue: "The dream experience is so short, while the world always exists. The dream experience was limited to me, but the world is felt and seen not only by me, but by so many, and we cannot call such a world non-existent," the argument called *srishti-drishti vada* is addressed and they are told: "God first created such and such a thing, out of such and such an element, and then something else and so forth." That alone will satisfy this class. Their mind is otherwise not satisfied and they ask themselves: "How can all geography, all maps, all sciences, stars, planets, and the rules governing or relating to them all be totally untrue?" To such it is best to say: "Yes, God created all this and so you see it."

'Dr. Masalavala objected: "But all these teachings cannot be true. Only one doctrine can be true."

'Bhagavan said: "All these viewpoints are only to suit the capacity of the learner. The absolute can only be one." '[1]

[1] D.D., II, p. 186

However, although Bhagavan approved of other paths for those who could not follow Self-enquiry, he said to the present writer: *'All other methods lead up to Self-enquiry.'* If a devotee of his found that some other, less direct path served him better, Bhagavan would guide him on this until he could gradually bring him to Self-enquiry.

'Talking of the innumerable ways of different seekers after God, Bhagavan said: "Each should be allowed to go his own way, the way for which alone he may be built. It will not do to convert him to another path by violence. The Guru will go with the disciple along his own path and then gradually turn him into the supreme path when the time is ripe. Suppose a car is going at top speed. To stop it and to turn it at once would lead to a crash." '[1]

Other methods are not necessarily exclusive of Self-enquiry; in fact some of them may very well be combined with it.

SAT SANG

The greatest of all aids to Self-realization is the presence of a Realized Man. This is called Sat Sang, which means literally fellowship with Being. Even here Bhagavan would sometimes explain that the real 'Being' is the Self and therefore no physical form is needed for Sat Sang. Nevertheless, he often dwelt on its benefits.

'Association with Sages who have realized the Truth removes material attachments; on these attachments being removed, the attachments of the mind are also destroyed. Those whose attachments of mind are thus destroyed become one with That which is Motionless. They attain Liberation while yet alive. Cherish association with such Sages.

'That Supreme State which is obtained here and now as a result of association with Sages, and realized through the deep

[1] D.D., II, p. 53

meditation of Self-enquiry in contact with the Heart, cannot be gained with the aid of a guru or through knowledge of the scriptures, or by spiritual merit, or by any other means.

'If association with Sages is obtained, to what purpose are the various methods of self-discipline? Tell me, of what use is a fan when the cool, gentle south wind is blowing? The heat of mental and bodily excitement is allayed by (the rays of) the moon; want and misery are removed by the kalpaka tree; sins are washed away by the sacred waters of the Ganges. All these afflictions are altogether banished by the mere *darshan* of the peerless Sage.

'Neither the holy waters of pilgrimage nor the images of gods made of earth and stone can stand comparison with the benign look of the Sage. These purify one only after countless days of grace, but no sooner does the Sage bestow his gracious glance than he purifies one.'[1]

It should be mentioned that these five verses were not actually composed by Bhagavan but translated from Sanskrit for inclusion in his Supplementary Forty Verses. The statement in the second verse that such grace cannot be gained with the aid of a guru is using the word 'guru' in its lower sense of 'teacher'; otherwise it would have the same meaning as 'Sage' and the comparison would be pointless.

BREATH CONTROL

Breath control can have various meanings. It can be retention of breath, or regulation of breathing according to a definite rhythm, or merely watching the breathing and remaining attentive to it. The Maharshi often authorized the use of breath control, but did not as a rule specify what form it was to take—perhaps because those who asked his authorization were usually practising a form of it prescribed by some guru and merely wished to know whether they could continue to do so. He himself, although competent to authorize any practice, did not teach or prescribe the more technical forms of breath control.

[1] F.V.S., p. 71

'As there are elaborate treatises on the elements of *ashtanga yoga* only as much as is necessary is written here. Anyone who desires to know more must resort to a practising yogi with experience and learn from him in detail.'[1]

When he did specify what kind of breath control was to be practised it was usually just watching the breathing, the type which is least likely to be harmful if practised without guidance from a guru who specializes in this kind of technical, indirect path.

'Mr. Prasad asked whether the regular form of breath control is not better, in which breathing in, holding the breath, and breathing out are to the rhythm of 1 : 4 : 2. Bhagavan replied: "All such rhythms, sometimes regulated not by counting but by incantations, are helps for controlling the mind; that is all. Watching the breathing is also one form of breath control. Holding the breath is more violent and may be harmful when there is no proper guru to guide the practiser at every step; but merely watching the breathing is easier and involves no risk.'[2]

The Maharshi was careful in authorizing breath control to explain why it was used—that it was helpful simply as a step towards mind control.

'The principle underlying the system of yoga is that the source of thought is also the source of breath and the vital force; therefore if one of them is effectively controlled the other is also automatically brought under control.[3]

'The source of the mind is the same as that of the breath and vital forces. It is really the multitude of thoughts that constitute the mind; and the I-thought is the primal thought of the mind and is itself the ego. But breath too has its origin at the same place whence the ego rises. Therefore, when the mind subsides, breath and the vital forces also subside; and conversely when the latter subside, the former also subsides.

[1] S.E., p. 35   [2] D.D., II, p. 60   [3] S.I, p. 12

'Breath and vital forces are also described as the gross manifestations of the mind. Till the hour of death the mind sustains
and supports these forces in the physical body; and when life
becomes extinct the mind envelops them and carries them away.
During sleep, however, the vital forces continue to function,
although the mind is not manifest. This is according to the divine
law and is intended to protect the body and to remove any
possible doubt as to whether it is alive or dead while one is
asleep. Without such arrangement by nature sleeping bodies would
often be cremated alive. The vitality apparent in breathing is left
behind by the mind as a "watchman". But in the wakeful state
and in *samadhi*, when the mind subsides breath also subsides. For
this reason (because the mind has the sustaining and controlling
power over breath and vital forces and is therefore ulterior to
both of them) the practice of breath control is merely helpful in
subduing the mind but cannot bring about its final extinction.'[1]

It follows from this that breath control, as authorized by Sri
Bhagavan, is necessary only for those who cannot control the mind
directly.

D.: Is it necessary to control one's breath?
B.: Breath control is only an aid for diving inwards. One can
as well dive down by controlling the mind. On the mind being
controlled the breath is automatically controlled. There is no
need to practise breath control; mind control is enough. Breath
control is recommended for the person who cannot control his
mind directly.[2]

This implies that Sri Bhagavan did not authorize breath control
as an independent technique but only as an approach towards mind
control. In itself he warned that its effects were impermanent.

'For the subsidence of the mind there is no other means more
effective and adequate than Self-enquiry. Even though by other

---

[1] W., p. 43   [2] T., p. 448

means the mind subsides, that is only apparently so; it will rise again.

'For instance, the mind subsides by means of breath control; yet such subsidence lasts only so long as the control of breath and vital forces continues; and when they are released the mind also gets released and immediately, being externalized, it continues to wander through the force of subtle tendencies.'[1]

Therefore, those who use it on the path prescribed by the Maharshi should also know when to give it up.

B.: Breath control is a help in controlling the mind and is advised for such as find they cannot control the mind without some such aid. For those who can control their mind and concentrate, it is not necessary. It can be used at the beginning until one is able to control the mind but then it should be given up.[2]

Another reason for caution in the use of breath control is that it may lead to subtle experiences which can distract the seeker from his true goal. As will be shown in the next chapter, Bhagavan always warned against interest in powers and experiences or desire for them; he sometimes specifically connected this warning with the use of breath control.

B.: Breath control is also a help. It is one of the various methods that are intended to help us attain *ekagratha* or one-pointedness of mind. Breath control can also help to control the wandering mind and attain this one-pointedness and therefore it can be used. But one should not stop there. After obtaining control of the mind through breath control one should not rest content with any experiences which may accrue therefrom but should harness the controlled mind to the question, 'Who am I?' till the mind merges in the Self.[3]

---

[1] W., p. 42   [2] D.D., I, p. 11   [3] D.D., I, p. 4

ASANAS

It was usual for devotees of Bhagavan to sit cross-legged in meditation before him; but the more elaborate yogic postures of *asanas* were not practised. As explained in the previous chapter, such postures are less important in Self-enquiry than on a yogic path.

D.: A number of *asanas* (postures) are mentioned. Which of them is the best?

B.: One-pointedness of mind is the best posture.[1]

HATHA YOGA

B.: The hatha yogis claim to keep the body fit so that the enquiry may be effected without obstacles. They also say that life must be prolonged so that the enquiry may be carried to a successful end. Furthermore there are those who use various drugs (*kayakalpa*) to that end. Their favourite example is that the canvas must be perfect before the painting is begun. Yes, but which is the canvas and which the painting? According to them the body is the canvas and the inquiry into the Self the painting. But isn't the body itself a picture on the canvas of the Self?

D.: But hatha yoga is much spoken of as an aid.

B.: Yes. Even great pandits well versed in Vedanta continue the practice of it. Otherwise their minds will not subside. So you may say it is useful for those who cannot otherwise still the mind.[2]

LIGHT-GAZING

D.: Why should one not adopt other means, such as gazing at a light?

[1] T., p. 557 [2] T., p. 619

B.: Light-gazing stupefies the mind and produces catalepsy of the will for the time being but produces no permanent benefit.[1]

CONCENTRATION ON SOUND

There are those who concentrate on the hearing of a sound—not any physical sound but sound from the subtle plane. The Maharshi did not disapprove of this but reminded them to hold on to the Self and find out who it is that hears the sound. The concentration achieved is good but does not in itself lead far enough. Enquiry also is needed.

'A Gujerati gentleman said that he was concentrating on sound (*nada*) and desired to know if the method was right.'

B.: Meditation on *nada* is one of the various approved methods. Its adherents claim a very special virtue for it. According to them it is the easiest and most direct method. Just as a child is lulled to sleep by lullabies, so *nada* soothes one to the state of *samadhi*. Again, just as a king sends his state musicians to welcome his son on his return from a long journey, so also *nada* takes the devotee into the Lord's abode in a pleasing manner. *Nada* helps concentration, but after it begins to be felt, the practice should not be made an end in itself. *Nada* is not the objective; the subject should firmly be held. Otherwise a blank will result. Though the subject is there even in the blank one must remember his own self. *Nada Upasana* (meditation on sound) is good; it is better if associated with Self-enquiry.[2]

CONCENTRATION ON THE HEART OR BETWEEN THE EYEBROWS

Concentration on the point between the eyebrows is a yogic practice. Bhagavan recognized its efficacy, especially when combined with

[1] T., p. 27   [2] T., p. 148

incantation, but recommended concentration on the heart on the right side as being both safer and more effective.

'A Maharashtra lady of middle age, who had studied Jnaneswari and Vichara Sagara, and was practising concentration between the eyebrows, had felt shivering and fear and did not progress. She required guidance. The Maharshi told her not to forget the seer. The sight is fixed between the eyebrows, but the seer is not kept in view. If the seer be always remembered it will be all right.[1]

'A visitor said: We are asked to concentrate on the spot in the forehead between the eyebrows. Is that right?'

B.: Everyone is aware that he is. Yet one ignores that awareness and goes about in search of God. What is the use of fixing one's attention between the eyebrows? The aim of such advice is to help the mind to concentrate. It is one of the forcible methods to check the mind and prevent its dissipation. The mind is forcibly directed into one channel and this is a help to concentration. But the method of realization is the enquiry 'Who am I?' The present trouble affects the mind and it can only be removed by the mind.[2]

D.: Sri Bhagavan speaks of the Heart as the seat of Consciousness and as identical with the Self. What exactly does the word 'Heart' signify?

B.: The question about the Heart arises because you are interested in seeking the source of Consciousness. To all deep-thinking minds, the enquiry about the 'I' and its nature has an irresistible fascination. Call it by any name, God, Self, the Heart or the seat of Consciousness, it is all the same. The point to be grasped is this, that Heart means the very core of one's being, the centre without which there is nothing whatever.

D.: But Sri Bhagavan has specified a particular place for the

[1] T., p. 162 [2] T., p. 557

Heart within the physical body—that is in the chest, two digits to the right of the median.

B.: Yes, that is the centre of spiritual experience according to the testimony of Sages. The spiritual heart-centre is quite different from the blood-propelling, muscular organ known by the same name. The spiritual heart-centre is not an organ of the body. All that you can say of the heart is that it is the core of your being. That with which you are really identical (as the word in Sanskrit literally means) whether you are awake, asleep or dreaming, whether you are engaged in work or immersed in *samadhi*.

D.: In that case, how can it be localized in any part of the body? Fixing a place for the Heart would imply setting physiological limitations to That which is beyond space and time.

B.: That is right. But the person who puts the question about the position of the Heart considers himself as existing with or in the body. While putting the question now, would you say that your body alone is here but that you are speaking from somewhere else? No, you accept your bodily existence. It is from this point of view that any reference to a physical body comes to be made. Truly speaking, pure Consciousness is indivisible; it is without parts. It has no form or shape, no within or without. There is no right or left. . . . Pure Consciousness—which is the Heart—includes all; and nothing is outside or apart from it. That is the ultimate truth.

D.: How shall I understand Sri Bhagavan's statement that the experience of the heart-centre is at that particular place in the chest?

B.: Pure Consciousness wholly unrelated to the physical body and transcending the mind is a matter of direct experience. Sages know their bodiless, eternal existence, just as an unrealized man knows his bodily existence. But the experience of Consciousness can be with bodily awareness as well as without it. In the bodiless experience of Pure Consciousness the Sage is beyond time and space, and no question about the position of the Heart can arise at all. Since, however, the physical body cannot subsist (with life) apart from Consciousness, bodily awareness has to be sustained by pure Consciousness. The former, by nature, is limited and can never be co-extensive with the latter which is Infinite and Eternal. Body-consciousness is merely a miniature reflection of the pure Consciousness with which the Sage has realized his identity. For him, therefore, body-consciousness is only a reflected ray, as it were, of the Self-effulgent, infinite Consciousness which is himself. It is in this sense alone that the Sage is aware of his bodily existence.

D.: For men like me, who have neither the direct experience of the Heart nor the consequent recollection, the matter seems to be somewhat difficult to grasp. About the position of the Heart itself, perhaps, we must depend upon some sort of guesswork.

B.: If the determination of the position of the Heart is to depend on guesswork even in the case of the unrealized, the question is surely not worth much consideration. No, it is not on guesswork that you have to depend, it is an unerring intuition.

D.: Who has the intuition?

B.: All people.

D.: Does Bhagavan credit me with an intuitive knowledge of the Heart?

B.: No, not of the Heart, but of the position of the Heart in relation to your identity.

D.: Sri Bhagavan says that I intuitively know the position of the Heart in the physical body?

B.: Why not?

D. (pointing to himself)*:* It is to me personally that Bhagavan is referring?

B.: Yes. That is the intuition! How did you refer to yourself by gesture just now? Did you not put your finger on the right side of the chest? That is exactly the place of the heart-centre.

D.: So then, in the absence of direct knowledge of the heart-centre, I have to depend on this intuition?

B.: What is wrong with it? When a schoolboy says: 'It is I who did the sum correctly', or when he asks you: 'Shall I run and get the book for you?', would he point to the head that did the sum correctly or to the legs that will swiftly get you that book? No, in both cases his finger is pointed quite naturally towards the right side of the chest, thus giving innocent expression to the profound truth that the source of 'I'-ness in him is there. It is an unerring intuition that makes him refer to himself, to the Heart which is the Self, in that way. The act is quite involuntary and universal, that is to say, it is the same in the case of every individual. What stronger proof than this do you require about the position of the Heart-centre in the physical body?

D.: But the question is which is the correct view of the two, namely: (1) that the centre of spiritual experience is the place between the eyebrows, (2) that it is the Heart.

B.: For the purpose of practice you may concentrate between the eyebrows if you like; it would then be *bhavana* or imaginative contemplation of the mind; whereas the supreme state of *anubhava* or Realization, with which you become wholly identified and in which your individuality is completely dissolved, transcends the mind. Then, there can be no objectified centre to be experienced by you as a subject distinct and separate from it.

D.: I would like to put my question in slightly different words. Can the place between the eyebrows be said to be the seat of the Self?

B.: You agree that the Self is the ultimate source of Consciousness and that it subsists equally during all the three states of mind. But see what happens when a person in meditation is overcome by sleep. As the first symptom of sleep his head begins to nod; but this could not happen if the Self were situated between the eyebrows, that centre cannot be called its seat without implying that the Self often forsakes its own place, which is absurd. The fact is the *sadhaka* may have his experience at any centre or *chakra* on which he concentrates his mind, but that does not make such a centre the seat of the Self. . . .

D.: Since Bhagavan says that the Self may function at any of the centres or *chakras* while its seat is in the Heart, is it not possible that by the practice of intense concentration or *dhyana* between the eyebrows this centre may itself become the seat of the Self?

B.: As long as it is merely the stage of practice of concentration in order to control your attention at one spot, any consideration about the seat of the Self would merely be theorization. You consider yourself the subject, the seer, and the place whereon you fix the attention becomes the object seen. This is merely *bhavana*. When, on the contrary, you see the Seer himself, you merge in the Self, you become one with it; that is the Heart.

D.: Then, is the practice of concentration between the eyebrows advisable?

B.: The final result of the practice of any kind of *dhyana* is that the object on which the aspirant fixes his mind ceases to exist as distinct and separate from the subject. Subject and object become one Self and that is the Heart. The practice of concentration on the centre between the eyebrows is one of the methods of training, and thereby thoughts are effectively controlled for the time being. The reason is that all thought is an outer activity of the mind; and thought, in the first instance, follows sight, physical or mental. It is important, however, that this practice of fixing one's attention between the eyebrows should be accompanied by incantations. Because next in importance to the eye of the mind is the ear of the mind (that is mental visualization of speech), either to control and thereby strengthen the mind, or to distract and thereby dissipate it. Therefore, while fixing the mind's eye on a centre, as, for instance, between the eyebrows, you should also practise the mental articulation of a Divine Name or incantation. Otherwise you will soon lose hold on the object of concentration. This kind of practice leads to the identification of the Name, Word or Self—whatever you may call it— with the centre selected for the purpose of meditation. Pure Consciousness, the Self or the Heart is the final Realization.[1]

[1] M.G., II, p. 68

THE SAHASRARA

Tantric paths teach the gradual uncoiling of the Kundalini or spiritual current in a man. As it uncoils and rises upwards, it enfranchises a series of *chakras* or spiritual centres in the body, each bestowing its own powers and perceptions until it culminates in the *Sahasrara* or thousand-petalled lotus in the brain or the crown of the head. When asked about this, Bhagavan replied that, whatever the experience may be, the ultimate seat of the Self, and therefore of Realization, is the Heart.

D.: Why doesn't Sri Bhagavan direct us to practise concentration on some particular centre or *chakra?*

B.: The Yoga Sastras say that the *Sahasrara* or brain is the seat of the Self. The *Purusha Sukta* declares that the Heart is its seat. To enable the aspirant to steer clear of any possible doubt, I tell him to take up the thread or the clue of 'I'-ness and follow it to its source. Because, firstly it is impossible for anybody to entertain any doubt about this 'I' notion; secondly, whatever be the means adopted, the final goal is Realization of the source of I-am-ness, which is what you begin from in your experience. If you, therefore, practise Self-enquiry you will reach the Heart which is the Self.[1]

D.: Does the *jivanadi* (subtle nerve column) really exist or is it a figment of the imagination?

B.: The yogis say that there is a *nadi* called the *jivanadi, atmanadi* or *paranadi.* The Upanishads speak of a centre from which thousands of *nadis* branch off. Some locate this in the brain and others in other places. The Garbhopanishad traces the formation of the foetus and the growth of the child in the womb. The ego is considered to enter the child through the fontanelle in the seventh month of its growth. In evidence thereof it is pointed out that the fontanelle is tender in a baby and is also seen

[1] M.G., II, p. 78

to pulsate. It takes some months for it to ossify. Thus the ego comes from above, enters through the fontanelle and works through thousands of *nadis*, which are spread over the whole body. Therefore the seeker of truth must concentrate on the *sahasrara*, that is the brain, in order to regain his source. Breath control is said to help the yogi to rouse the *Kundalini-Shakti* which lies coiled in the solar plexus. The shakti rises through a nerve called the *sushumna*, which is embedded in the core of the spinal cord and extends to the brain.

'If one concentrates on the *sahasrara* there is no doubt that the ecstasy of *samadhi* ensues. The *vasanas*, that is the latencies, are, however, not destroyed. The yogi is therefore bound to wake up from *samadhi* because the release from bondage is not yet accomplished. He must still try to eradicate the *vasanas* in order that the latencies yet inherent in him may not disturb the peace of his *samadhi*. So he passes down from the *sahasrara* to the heart through what is called the *jivanadi* which is only a continuation of the *sushumna*. The *sushumna* is thus a curve. It starts from the solar plexus, rises through the spinal cord to the brain and from there bends down and ends in the heart. When the yogi has reached the heart, the *samadhi* becomes permanent. Thus we see that the heart is the final centre.

'Some Upanishads also speak of a hundred and one *nadis* which spread from the heart, one of them being the vital *nadi*. If the ego descends from above and is reflected in the brain, as the yogis say, there must be a reflecting surface. This must also be capable of limiting the Infinite Consciousness to the limits of the body. In short, the Universal Being becomes limited as an ego. Such a reflecting medium is furnished by the aggregate of *vasanas* of the individual. It acts like the water in a pot which reflects an object. If the pot is drained of its water there will be no reflection. The object will remain without being reflected. The object here is the Universal Being-Consciousness which is all-pervading and therefore immanent in all. It need not be cognized by reflection alone. It is self-resplendent. Therefore, the seekers' aim must be to drain away the *vasanas* from the heart and let no reflecting consciousness obstruct the light of the Eternal Consciousness. This is achieved by the search for the origin of the ego and by diving into the heart. This is the direct path to Self-realization. One who adopts it need not worry about *nadis*, brain, *sushumna*, *kundalini*, breath control and the six yogic centres.

'The Self does not come from anywhere or enter the body through the crown of the head. It is as it is, ever-shining, ever steady, unmoving and unchanging. The changes which are noticed are not inherent in the Self, for the Self abides in the heart and is self-luminous like the sun. The changes are seen in its light. The relation between the Self and the body or the mind may be compared to that of a clear crystal and its background. If the crystal is placed against a red flower it shines red, if against green it shines green, and so on. The individual confines himself to the limits of the changeable body or of the mind which derives its existence from the unchanging Self. All that is necessary is to give up this mistaken identity and, that done, the ever-shining Self will be seen to be the single, non-dual Reality.'[1]

SILENCE

On the whole the Maharshi did not approve of vows of silence. If the mind is controlled, useless speech will be avoided; but abjuring speech will not quieten the mind. The effect cannot produce the cause.

D.: Isn't a vow of silence helpful?

B.: A vow is only a vow. It may help meditation to some extent; but what is the use of keeping the mouth shut and letting the mind run riot? If the mind is engaged in meditation, what need is there for speech? Nothing is as good as meditation. What is the use of a vow of silence if one is engrossed in activity?[2]

---

[1] T., p. 616   [2] W, pp. 43-4

DIET

Although in general attaching little importance to physical aids to meditation, the Maharshi was insistent on the advantages of limiting oneself to *sattvic*, that is vegetarian and non-stimulating food.

'Regulation of diet, restricting it to *sattvic* food, taken in moderate quantities, is the best of all rules of conduct and the most conducive to the development of *sattvic* (pure) qualities of mind. These in turn help one in the practice of Self-enquiry.'[1]

The following is the conclusion of 'Self-enquiry', the first book that he wrote:

'It is within our power to adopt a simple and nutritious diet and, with earnest and incessant endeavour, to eradicate the ego—the cause of all misery—by stopping all mental activity born of the ego.

'Can obsessing thoughts arise without the ego, or can there be illusion apart from such thoughts?'[2]:

He confirmed this also when asked by devotees.

D.: Are there any aids to (1) concentration, and (2) casting off distractions?

B.: Physically, the digestive and other organs are to be kept free from irritation. Therefore food is regulated both in quantity and quality. Non-irritants are eaten, avoiding chillies, excess of salt, onions, wine, opium, etc. Avoid constipation, drowsiness and excitement and all foods which induce them. Mentally, take interest in one thing and fix the mind on it. Let that interest be self-absorbing to the exclusion of everything else. This is dispassion (*vairagya*) and concentration.[3]

[1] T., p. 371   [2] S.E., p. 38   [3] T., p. 28

'Mrs. Piggot returned from Madras for a further visit and asked questions concerning diet.'

Mrs. P.: What diet is suitable for a person engaged in spiritual practice?
B.: Sattvic food in moderate quantities.
Mrs. P.: What food is *sattvic?*
B.: Bread, fruit, vegetables, milk and such things.
Mrs. P.: Some people in the North eat fish. Is that permissible?

To this question Bhagavan did not reply. He was always reluctant to criticize others and this question was inviting him either to do so or to change what he had said.

Mrs. P.: We Europeans are accustomed to a particular diet and change of diet affects the health and weakens the mind. Isn't it necessary to keep up physical health?
B.: Quite necessary. The weaker the body the stronger the mind grows.
Mrs. P.: In the absence of our usual diet our health suffers and the mind loses strength.

It will be noticed that Bhagavan and Mrs. Piggot were using the term 'strength of mind' in different meanings. By 'strong' Bhagavan was meaning 'ungovernable', whereas Mrs. Piggot was meaning 'powerful'. Therefore the next question, which enabled her to put her point of view.

B.: What do you mean by 'strength of mind'?
Mrs. P.: The power to eliminate worldly attachment.
B.: The quality of one's food influences the mind. The mind feeds on the food consumed.
Mrs. P.: Really! But how can Europeans accommodate themselves to *sattvic* food?
B. (turning to Mr. Evans-Wentz): You have been taking our food. Does it inconvenience you at all?

E.W.: No, because I am accustomed to it.

B.: Custom is only an adjustment to environment. It is the mind that matters. The fact is that the mind has been trained to find certain foods good and palatable. The necessary food value is obtainable in vegetarian as well as non-vegetarian food; only the mind desires the sort of food that it is used to and considers palatable.

Mrs. P.: Do these restrictions apply to the realized man also?

B.: He is stabilized and not influenced by the food he takes.[1]

It was very characteristic of Bhagavan that, although he would answer questions about diet quite firmly when asked, he would not enjoin a vegetarian diet on any devotee who did not ask him. It was also characteristic that, under his silent influence, it would sometimes happen that one who did not ask would gradually begin to feel an aversion to meat-food and an inclination to change over to a purer diet.

Just as Bhagavan disapproved of all extremes, he disapproved of fasting.

D.: Can fasting help towards Realization?

B.: Yes, but it is only a temporary help. It is mental fasting that is the real aid. Fasting is not an end in itself. There must be spiritual development at the same time. Absolute fasting weakens the mind too and leaves you without sufficient strength for the spiritual quest. Therefore eat in moderation and continue the quest.

D.: They say that ten days after breaking a month's fast the mind becomes pure and steady and remains so for ever.

B.: Yes, but only if the spiritual quest has been kept up right through the fast.[2]

CELIBACY

There is no need to say much about celibacy, since it has been dealt with in an earlier chapter. It is normal in India that all those who do

[1] T., p. 22 [2] T., p. 170

not renounce the world to become sadhus marry, and Bhagavan discouraged renunciation. He never enjoined celibacy and he showed interest in births and marriages among the devotees.

BHAKTI

We come now to *bhakti marga*, the path of love and devotion, worship and surrender. This is usually considered the very antithesis of Self-enquiry, since it is based on the presumption of duality, of worshipper and worshipped, lover and beloved, whereas Self-enquiry presumes non-duality. Therefore theorists are apt to presume that if one is based on truth the other must be based on error, and in expounding one they only too often condemn the other. Bhagavan not only recognized both these paths but guided his followers on them both. He often said:

'There are two ways; ask yourself, "Who am I?" or surrender.' Many of his followers chose the latter way.

D.: What is unconditional surrender?

B.: If one surrenders completely there will be no one left to ask questions or to be considered. Either the thoughts are eliminated by holding on to the root thought, 'I', or one surrenders unconditionally to the Higher Power. These are the only two ways to Realization.[1]

Self-enquiry dissolves the ego by looking for it and finding it to be non-existent, whereas devotion surrenders it; therefore both come to the same ego-free goal, which is all that is required.

B.: There are only two ways to conquer destiny or to be independent of it. One is to enquire whose this destiny is and discover that only the ego is bound by it and not the Self, and that the ego is non-existent. The other way is to kill the ego by completely surrendering to the Lord, realizing one's helplessness and saying all the time: 'Not I, but Thou, O Lord!', giving up

[1] T., p. 321

all sense of 'I' and 'mine' and leaving it to the Lord to do what he likes with you. Surrender can never be regarded as complete so long as the devotee wants this or that from the Lord. True surrender is the love of God for the sake of love and nothing else, not even for the sake of salvation. In other words, complete effacement of the ego is necessary to conquer destiny, whether you achieve this effacement through Self-enquiry or through *bhakti marga*.[1]

'The spark of spiritual knowledge (*Jnana*) will consume all creation like a mountain of gunpowder. Since all the countless worlds are built upon the weak or non-existent foundations of the ego, they all disintegrate when the atom-bomb of knowledge falls on them. All talk of surrender is like stealing sugar from a sugar image of Ganesha and then offering it to the same Ganesha. You say that you offer up your body and soul and all your possessions to God, but were they yours to offer? At best you can say: "I wrongly imagined till now that all these, which are Yours, were mine. Now I realize that they are Yours, and shall no longer act as though they were mine." And this knowledge that there is nothing but God or Self, that "I" and "mine" do not exist and that only the Self exists is *Jnana*'[2]

He often explained, however, that true devotion is devotion to the Self and therefore comes to the same as Self-enquiry.

'It is enough that one surrenders oneself. Surrender is giving oneself up to the original cause of one's being. Do not delude yourself by imagining this source to be some God outside you. One's source is within oneself. Give yourself up to it. That means that you should seek the source and merge in it. Because you imagine yourself to be out of it, you raise the question, "Where is the source?" Some contend that just as sugar cannot taste its own sweetness but there must be someone to taste and enjoy it, so an individual cannot both be the Supreme and also enjoy the Bliss of that State; therefore the individuality must be maintained

[1] D.D., I, p. 57   [2] D.D., II, p. 53

separate from the Godhead in order to make enjoyment possible. But is God insentient like sugar? How can one surrender oneself and yet retain one's individuality for supreme enjoyment? Furthermore they also say that the soul, on reaching the divine region and remaining there, serves the supreme Being. Can the sound of the word "service" deceive the Lord? Does He not know? Is He waiting for these people's services? Would He not—the Pure Consciousness—ask in turn: "Who are you apart from Me that presume to serve Me?"

'If, on the other hand, you merge in the Self there will be no individuality left. You will become the Source itself. In that case, what is surrender? Who is to surrender what and to whom? This constitutes devotion, wisdom and Self-enquiry. Among the Vaishnavites, too, Saint Nammalwar says: "I was in a maze, clinging to 'I' and 'mine'; I wandered without knowing myself. On realizing myself I understand that I myself am You and that 'mine' (that is, my possessions) is only Yours." Thus, you see, devotion is nothing more than knowing oneself. The school of qualified monism also admits it. Still, adhering to their traditional doctrine, they persist in affirming that individuals are part of the Supreme—his limbs as it were. Their traditional doctrine says also that the individual soul should be made pure and then surrendered to the Supreme; then the ego is lost and one goes to the region of Vishnu after death; then finally there is the enjoyment of the Supreme (or the Infinite). To say that one is apart from the primal source is itself a pretension; to add that one divested of the ego becomes pure and yet retains individuality only to enjoy or serve the Supreme is a deceitful stratagem. What duplicity this is—first to appropriate what is really His, and then pretend to experience or serve Him! Is not all this known to Him?"[1]

It is obvious that surrender in the total uncompromising sense in which Bhagavan demands it is not easy.

[1] T., p. 208

'As often as one tries to surrender, the ego raises its head and one has to try to suppress it. Surrender is not an easy thing. Killing the ego is not an easy thing. It is only when God Himself by His Grace draws the mind inwards that complete surrender can be achieved.'[1]

'Dr. Syed asked Bhagavan: Doesn't total or complete surrender imply that even desire for liberation or God should be given up?'

B.: Complete surrender does imply that you should have no desire of your own, that God's will alone is your will and you have no will of your own.

Dr. S.: Now that I am satisfied on that point, I want to know what are the steps by which I can achieve surrender?

B.: There are two ways; one is looking into the source of the 'I' and merging into that source; the other is feeling 'I am helpless by myself, God alone is all-powerful and except for throwing myself completely on Him there is no other means of safety for me,' and thus gradually developing the conviction that God alone exists and the ego does not count. Both methods lead to the same goal. Complete surrender is another name for *Jnana* or Liberation.[2]

However, partial surrender can come first and gradually become more and more complete.

D.: I find surrender impossible.

B.: Complete surrender is impossible in the beginning but partial surrender is possible for all. In course of time that will lead to complete surrender.[3]

The dualists may however object that the devotional path approved by Bhagavan is not that which they have in mind, since theirs presupposes the permanent duality of God and worshipper. In such cases, as in the last sentence of the following dialogue, Bhagavan would

[1] D.D., I, p. 54 [2] D.D., II, p. 175 [3] T., p. 244

raise the discussion above theory, bidding them first achieve the surrender to a separate God, of which they spoke, and then see whether they had any further doubts.

'The state we call realization is simply being oneself, not knowing anything or becoming anything. If one has realized, he is that which alone is and which alone has always been. He cannot describe that state. He can only be that. Of course we talk loosely of Self-realization for want of a better term, but how is one to realize or make real that which alone is real? What we all are doing is to realize or regard as real what is unreal. This habit has to be given up. All spiritual effort under all systems is directed only to this end. When we give up regarding the unreal as real, then Reality alone will remain and we shall be That.

'The Swami replied: "This exposition is all right in the framework of non-duality, but there are other schools which do not insist on the disappearance of the triad of knower, knowledge and known as the condition for Self-realization. There are schools which believe in the existence of two and even three eternal entities. There is the *bhakta*, for instance. In order that he may worship there must be a God." '

B.: Whoever objects to his having a separate God to worship so long as he needs one? Through devotion he develops until he comes to feel that God alone exists, and that he himself does not count. He comes to a stage when he says, 'Not I but Thou; not my will but Thine.' When that stage is reached, which is called complete surrender in *bhakti marga*, one finds that effacement of the ego is attainment of the Self. We need not quarrel whether there are two entities or more or only one. Even according to dualists and according to *bhakti marga* complete surrender is necessary. Do that first and then see for yourself whether the one Self alone exists or whether there are two or more.

'Bhagavan further added: "Whatever may be said to suit the different capacities of different men, the truth is that the state of

Self-realization must be beyond the triad of knower, knowledge and known. The Self is the Self; that is all that can be said of it."

'The Swami then asked whether a *Jnani* could retain his body after attaining Self-realization. He added: "It is said that the impact of Self-realization is so forceful that the weak physical body cannot bear it for more than twenty-one days at the longest." Bhagavan replied: "What is your idea of a *Jnani*? Is he the body or something different? If he is something apart from the body, how can he be affected by the body? Books speak of different kinds of Liberation, *videhamukti* (without body) and *jivanmukti* (with body). There may be different stages on the path but there are no degrees of Liberation." '[1]

Sometimes Bhagavan was asked how the paths of love and knowledge could be the same since love postulates duality.

D.: Love postulates duality. How can the Self be the object of love?
B.: Love is not different from the Self. Love of an object is of a lower type and cannot endure, whereas the Self is Love. God is Love.[2]

For those whose temperament and state of development demanded it, the Maharshi approved of ritualistic worship, which usually accompanies a devotional path.

'A visitor said to Bhagavan: "Priests prescribe various rituals and forms of worship and people are told that it is a sin not to observe them. Is there any need for such ritual and ceremonial worship?" '
B.: Yes, such worship is also necessary. It may not help you, but that does not mean that it is necessary for no one and is no good at all. What is necessary for the infant is not necessary for the graduate. But even the graduate has to make use of the

[1] D.D., II, p. 195 [2] T., p. 433

alphabet he learnt in the infant class. He knows its full use and significance.[1]

Worship might also take the form of concentration on one of the Hindu gods, that is one of the modes in which Hindus conceive of God.

D.: What are the steps of practical training?

B.: It depends on the qualifications and nature of the seeker.

D.: I worship an idol.

B.: Go on doing so. It leads to concentration of mind. Get one-pointed. All will come right in the end. People think that Liberation (*moksha*) is somewhere outside them to be sought for. They are wrong. It is only knowing the Self in you. Concentrate and you will get it. It is your mind that is the cycle of births and deaths (*samsara*).

D.: My mind is very unsteady. What should I do?

B.: Fix your attention on any single thing and try to hold on to it. Everything will come right.

D.: I find concentration difficult.

B.: Keep on practising and your concentration will come to be as easy as breathing. That will be the crown of your achievement.[2]

However, he did not approve of the desire to see visions—or, in fact, any desire at all, even the desire for rapid realization.

'Miss Uma Devi, a Polish lady who had become a Hindu, said to Sri Bhagavan: Once before I told Sri Bhagavan how I had a vision of Siva at about the time I became a Hindu. A similar experience occurred to me at Courtallam. These visions are momentary, but they are blissful. I want to know how they can be made permanent and continuous. Without Siva there is no life in what I see around me. I am so happy to think of Him. Please tell me how I can make the vision of Him continuous.'

[1] D.D II, p. 100   [2] T., p. 31

B.: You speak of a vision of Siva, but a vision always presumes an object. That implies the existence of a subject. The value of the vision is the same as that of the seer. That is to say, the nature of the vision is on the same plane as that of the seer. Appearance implies disappearance also. Therefore a vision can never be eternal. But Siva is eternal. The vision of Siva implies the existence of the eyes to see it, of the intellect behind the sight and finally of Consciousness underlying the seer. This vision is not as real as one imagines it to be, because it is not intimate and inherent; it is not first hand. It is the result of several successive phases of Consciousness. Consciousness alone does not vary. It is eternal. It is Siva. A vision implies someone to see it, but this someone cannot deny the existence of the Self. There is no moment when the Self as Consciousness does not exist nor can the seer remain apart from Consciousness. This Consciousness is the Eternal Being and is only Being. The seer cannot see himself. Does he deny his existence because he cannot see himself as he sees a vision? No; so the true vision does not mean seeing but BE-ing. TO BE is to realize—Hence 'I AM THAT I AM'. I AM Siva. Nothing else can be without Him. Everything has its being in Siva, because of Siva. Therefore enquire: 'Who am I?' Sink deep within and abide as the Self. That is Siva as BE-ing. Do not expect to have visions of Him repeated. What is the difference between the objects you see and Siva? He is both subject and object. You cannot be without Siva. Siva is always realized here and now. If you think you have not realized Him you are wrong. That is the obstacle to realizing Him. Give up that thought also and realization is there.

D.: Yes, but how shall I effect it as quickly as possible?

B.: That is another obstacle to Realization. Can there be an individual without Siva? Even now He is you. There is no question of time. If there were a moment of non-realization, the question of realization could arise. But you cannot be without Him. He is already realized, ever realized and never non-realized. Surrender to Him and abide by His will, whether he appears or vanishes; await His pleasure. If you ask Him to do as you please, it is not surrender but command. You cannot have Him obey you and yet think you have surrendered. He knows what is best and when and how. Leave everything entirely to Him. The burden is His.

'You have no longer any cares. All your cares are His. That is surrender. That is *bhakti.*[1]'

D.: A vision of God is something glorious.

B.: A vision of God is only a vision of the Self objectified as the God of your particular faith. What you have to do is to know the Self.[2]

'Bhagavan was often heard to say: "To know God is to love God, therefore the paths of *jnana* and *bhakti* (knowledge and devotion) come to the same." '

JAPA

Japa, that is the use of incantations and invocations of a Divine Name, is one of the most widely practised techniques of spiritual training. It has particular affinity with *bhakti* paths of love and devotion. The Maharshi approved of it, subject, of course, to the condition illustrated in the story of the king and his minister on page 96, that the person who practised any incantation had been duly authorized to do so by a qualified guru. He himself occasionally authorized the use of invocations, but very seldom.

'The point is to keep out all other thoughts except the one thought of OM or Ram or God. All incantations and invocations help to do that.'[3]

The more devotion there is behind the words the better this is accomplished, and therefore the more effective is the incantation.

D.: When I invoke the Divine Name for an hour or more I fall into a state like sleep. On waking up I recollect that my invocation has been interrupted, so I try again.

[1] T., p. 450   [2] T., p. 621   [3] D.D., II, p. 101

B.: 'Like sleep', that is right. It is the natural state. Because
you now identify yourself with the ego, you look upon the natural
state as something which interrupts your work. So you must
have the experience repeated until you realize that it is your
natural state. You will then find that the invocation is extraneous,
but still it will go on automatically. Your present doubt is due to
false identification of yourself with the mind that makes the
invocation. Invocation really means clinging to one thought to
the exclusion of all others. That is the purpose of it. It leads to
absorption which ends in Self-realization or *Jnana.*

D.: How should I practise invocation?

B.: One should not use the name of God mechanically and
superficially without a feeling of devotion. When one uses the
name of God one should call on Him with yearning and un-
reservedly surrender oneself to Him. Only after such surrender
is the name of God constantly with you.[1]

In its early stages an incantation may even be accompanied by
visualization of the form of a Guru or of a mythological form of God.

D.: My practice has been continuous invocation of the names
of God while breathing in and of the name of Sai Baba while
breathing out. Simultaneously with this I see the form of Baba
always. Even in Bhagavan I see Baba. The external appearances
are also much alike. Bhagavan is thin. Baba was a little stout.
Should I continue this method or change it? Something within
tells me that if I stick to name and form I shall never get beyond
them but I can't understand what further to do if I give them up.
Will Bhagavan please enlighten me?

B.: You may continue with your present method. When the
japa becomes continuous all other thoughts cease and one is in
one's real nature which is invocation or absorption. We turn our
minds outwards to things of the world and are therefore not
aware that our real nature is always invocation. When by conscious effort, or invocation, or meditation as we call it, we prevent

[1] M.G., I, p. 24

our minds from thinking of other things, then what remains is our real nature, which is invocation. So long as you think you are the name and form, you can't escape name and form in invocation also. When you realize you are not name and form the name and form will drop off themselves. No other effort is necessary. Invocation or meditation will lead to it naturally and as a matter of course. Invocation which is now regarded as the means will then be found to be the goal. There is no difference between God and His name.[1]

As the above passage indicates, incantation merges with *dhyana,* which, for want of a better word, is translated 'meditation'. For this reason, silent incantation is better than vocal, being more inward.

D.: Isn't mental invocation better than oral?

B.: Oral incantation consists of sounds. The sounds arise from thoughts, for one must think before one expresses one's thoughts in words. The thoughts form the mind. Therefore mental invocation is better than oral.

D.: Shouldn't we contemplate the invocation and repeat it orally also?

B.: When the invocation becomes mental where is the need for sound? On becoming mental it becomes contemplation. Meditation, contemplation and mental invocation are the same. When thoughts cease to be promiscuous and one thought persists to the exclusion of all others it is said to be contemplation. The object of invocation or meditation is to exclude varied thought and confine oneself to one. Then that thought too vanishes into its source, which is pure Consciousness or the Self. The mind first engages in invocation and then sinks into its own source.[2]

'This is certain: worship, incantations and meditation are performed respectively with the body, the voice and the mind and are in this ascending order of value.

'One can regard this eightfold universe as a manifestation of

God; and whatever worship is performed in it is excellent as worship of God.

'The repetition aloud of His name is better than praise. Better still is its faint murmur. But the best is repetition with the mind—and that is meditation, above referred to.

'Better than such broken thoughts (meditation) is its steady and continuous flow like the flow of oil or of a perennial stream.'[1]

KARMA MARGA

Little need be said here about *karma marga*, the path of action, since it has been dealt with in an earlier chapter. The Maharshi discouraged unnecessary activities on the one hand and the attempt to renounce activity on the other, enjoining performance of the necessary routine activities of life in a detached manner, simultaneously with the practice of enquiry or devotion.

D.: Swami, how can the grip of the ego be loosened?

B.: By not adding new *vasanas* (innate tendencies) to it.

D.: How does activity help? Will it not add to the already heavy load that has to be removed?

B.: Actions performed with no thought of the ego purify the mind and help to fix it in meditation.

D.: But suppose one were to meditate incessantly without activity?

B.: Try and see. Your innate tendencies will not let you. Meditation (*dhyana*) comes only step by step with the weakening of the innate tendencies by the Grace of the Guru.[2]

METHODS GRADED

Although the Maharshi recognized all methods, he graded them as more or less direct and effective, as is shown in the above quotation of verses 4–7 of the 'Essence of Instruction'. The following exposition also makes this clear.

[1] E.I., verses 4–7   [2] T., p. 80

'Examination of the ephemeral nature of external things leads to dispassion (*vairagya*). Hence enquiry is the first and most important step. When it becomes automatic it results in indifference to wealth, fame, ease, pleasure and so on. The "I"-thought is traced to the source of the "I" in the Heart, which is the final goal.

'However, if the aspirant is temperamentally unsuited for Self-enquiry he must develop devotion. It may be to God or Guru or mankind in general or ethical laws or even an ideal of beauty. As any of these takes possession of him other attachments grow weaker and dispassion develops. Attachment to the object of devotion grows until it dominates him completely, and with it grows concentration (*ekagrata*) with or without visions and direct aids.

'If neither enquiry nor devotion appeals to him, he can gain tranquillity by breath control. This is the way of yoga. If a man's life is in danger all his interest centres round the one point of saving it. If the breath is held the mind cannot afford to jump out at its beloved outer objects and does not do so. Therefore there is peace of mind as long as the breath is held. Since all one's attention is concentrated on the breath, other interests are abandoned. Then also, any passion results in irregular breathing. A paroxysm of joy is in fact as painful as one of grief, and both result in disturbed breathing. Real peace is happiness, and pleasures do not produce happiness.

'If the aspirant is unsuited to the first two methods by temperament and to the third on account of age or health, he must try *karma marga*, the path of good deeds and social service. His nobler instincts are thus developed and he derives impersonal happiness from his actions. His ego becomes less assertive and its good side is enabled to develop. He thus in course of time comes to be suited for one of the three former paths. Or his intuition may be developed by *karma marga* alone.'[1]

---

[1] T., p. 27

7

THE GOAL

D.: What is the purpose of Self-realization?

B.: Self-realization is the final goal and is itself the purpose.

D.: I mean, what use is it?

B.: Why do you ask about Self-realization? Why don't you rest content with your present state? It is evident that you are discontented and your discontent will come to an end if you realize yourself.[1]

The above question was seldom asked, because those who came to the Maharshi usually understood at least that the state of spiritual ignorance (or, as Christianity puts it, of 'fallen man') is undesirable and that Self-realization is the supreme goal. In the following dialogue the purpose is asked with more understanding and therefore the answer also goes deeper.

D.: What is the goal of this process?

B.: Realizing the Real.

D.: What is the nature of Reality?

B.: (*a*) Existence without beginning or end—eternal.

    (*b*) Existence everywhere, endless—infinite.

    (*c*) Existence underlying all forms, all changes, all forces, all matter and all spirit.

The many change and pass away, whereas the One always endures.

    (*d*) The one displaces the triads such as knower, know-

[1] T., p. 487

ledge and known. The triads are only appearances
in time and space, whereas the Reality lies beyond
and behind them. They are like a mirage over the
Reality. They are the result of delusion.

D.: If 'I' am also an illusion, who casts off the illusion?

B.: The 'I' casts off the illusion of 'I' and yet remains 'I'.
Such is the paradox of Self-realization. The Realized do not see
any contradiction in it.[1]

It is surprising how many philosophers and theologians have
failed to understand what is implied by Self-realization and have mis-
represented and even attacked or belittled it. All that it means, as
Bhagavan explains in the passage just quoted, is realizing Reality,
realizing what is. And Reality remains the same, eternal and unchanging, whether one realizes it or not. One can, of course, understand the annoyance and frustration of philosophers who wish to
grasp everything with the mind at being told that Reality lies beyond
and behind the triad of knower-knowledge-known, which is like a
mirage over it; for obviously the mirage cannot penetrate to that which
underlies it. That is why no easy answer can be given to them. Indeed,
Bhagavan did not on the whole approve of questions about the
meaning and nature of Realization, because his purpose was to help
the questioner and not to satisfy mental curiosity. He usually reminded people that what is needed is effort to attain Self-knowledge;
and when that is attained the questions will not arise.

'Some people who come here don't ask me about themselves
but about the *Jivanmukta*, liberated while still embodied. Does
he see the world? Is he subject to destiny? Can one be liberated
only after leaving the body or while yet alive? Should the body
of a Sage resolve itself into light or disappear from sight in a
miraculous way? Can one who leaves a corpse behind at death be
liberated? Their questions are endless. Why worry about all
these things? Does Liberation consist in knowing the answer to
these questions? So, I tell them, "Never mind about Liberation.
First find out whether there is such a thing as bondage. Examine
yourself first." '[2]

[1] T., p. 28   [2] T., p. 578

He sometimes pointed out that even to speak of Self-realization is a delusion—an illusory escape from an illusory prison.

B.: In a sense, speaking of Self-realization is a delusion. It is only because people have been under the delusion that the non-Self is the Self and the unreal the Real that they have to be weaned out of it by the other delusion called Self-realization; because actually the Self always is the Self and there is no such thing as realizing it. Who is to realize what, and how, when all that exists is the Self and nothing but the Self?[1]

One thing which impedes understanding, especially in theologians, is the contrast between Self-realization and sainthood and the mistaken idea that it may represent a difference between different religious traditions, one striving for sainthood and another for Realization. This idea is quite ungrounded. There have been saints in every religion, Hinduism as well as others. They differ very much among themselves, both in individual characteristics, from the rapturous to the serene, from the austere to the benign, from the subtle philosopher to the simple-minded, and also in degree of attainment; some of them possess supernatural powers, some are swept away in ecstatic bliss, some consume themselves in loving service to mankind; all have a purity beyond that of ordinary men. Their state may be called heavenly even while on earth. And yet all this falls short of Self-realization. All this is in the state of duality, where God or Self is the Other, where prayer is necessary, and revelation possible. In strict theory they are as far removed as the ordinary man from Self-realization, since there is no common measure between the Absolute and the conditioned, the Infinite and the limited. A million is no nearer to Infinity than a hundred. This complete gulf is illustrated by the Buddhist story of the man who wanders about the earth seeking for a lost jewel which all the time is on his brow. When at last it is pointed out to him, all his years of search and wandering have done nothing to bring him nearer to it. And yet, in actual fact, if he had not gone searching he would not have found it. And in actual fact the saint can be considered nearer to Realization than ordinary men, just as it is easier for an ordinary man to attain Realization than for a dog, although both alike are limited to the illusion of individual being.

[1] D.D., I, p. 61

There are stages of attainment of the saints, just as there is a hierarchy of heavens; and both of these correspond to the degrees of initiation in indirect spiritual paths. Bhagavan would answer questions about this when specifically asked, but did not usually speak of it, since his purpose was not to raise his followers from grade to grade of apparent reality but to direct them towards the one, eternal, universal Reality.

D.: Do we go to *Svarga* (heaven) as a result of our actions here?

B.: Heaven is as real as your present life. But if we ask who we are and discover the Self, what need is there to think of heaven?[1]

D.: Is *Vaikunta* (heaven) in the Supreme Self?

B.: Where is the Supreme Self or heaven unless in you.

D.: But heaven may appear to one involuntarily.

B.: Does this world appear voluntarily?[2]

Similarly he would briefly acknowledge grades of development in the individual but would not dwell on them.

'The yogic centres, counting from the bottom upwards, are a series of centres in the nervous system, each having its own kind of power or knowledge.'[3]

When someone told him about a present-day saint who was said to be constantly inspired by an Incarnation of God and to speak only as divinely directed and asked him whether this was true or not, replied:

'As true as all this that you see around you.'

For, as compared with the Self, neither this physical world nor any higher world is inherently real, just as, compared with infinity, a big number has no more meaning than a small one.

A saint may attain a lofty grade without ever conceiving of the ultimate Reality of Oneness or having only brief ecstatic intimations

[1] T., p. 31   [2] T., p. 385   [3] S.D.B., xviii

of it. That does not matter; the power of his purity and aspiration will eventually sweep him onwards either in this life or beyond.

For one who envisages the ultimate Goal and strives towards it there are no stages; either he is realized or he is not. About this Bhagavan spoke willingly and explicitly, because this was the path he enjoined.

'There are no stages in Realization or *Mukti*. There are no degrees of Liberation.'[1]

D.: There must be stage after stage of progress before attaining the Absolute. Are there different levels of Reality?

B.: There are no levels of Reality; there are only levels of experience for the individual, not of Reality. If anything can be gained which was not there before, it can also be lost, whereas the Absolute is eternal, here and now.[2]

However, although there are no stages of Self-realization there are what might be called pre-views, glimpses which are not yet stabilized or made permanent. Sometimes, indeed, these occur to people who, in this lifetime, have had no spiritual training at all. As the opacity of the aspirant's ego lessens with training in abnegation he becomes more liable to them. Even great mystic philosophers such as Plotinus or Meister Eckhart have, by their own admission, been dependent on them, not having attained to the permanent state of identity from which Bhagavan taught.

'Can a man become a high official merely by seeing one? He may become one if he strives and equips himself for the position. Similarly, can the ego, which is in bondage as the mind, become the Divine Self simply because it has once glimpsed that it is the Self? Is this not impossible without the destruction of the mind? Can a beggar become a king by merely visiting a king and declaring himself one?'[3]

D.: Can Self-realization be lost again after once being attained?

[1] D.D., II, p. 110 [2] T., p. 132 [3] S.E., p. 30

B.: Realization takes time to steady itself. The Self is certainly within the direct experience of everyone but not in the way people imagine. One can only say that it is as it is. Just as incantations or other devices can prevent fire from burning a man when otherwise it would do so, so *vasanas* (inherent tendencies impelling one to desire one thing and to shun another) can veil the Self when otherwise it would be apparent. Owing to the fluctuations of the *vasanas*, Realization takes time to steady itself. Spasmodic Realization is not enough to prevent re-birth, but it cannot become permanent as long as there are *vasanas*. In the presence of a great master, *vasanas* cease to be active and the mind becomes still so that *samadhi* (absorption in Realization) results, just as in the presence of various devices fire does not burn. Thus the disciple gains true knowledge and right experience in the presence of a master. But if this is to be established further effort is necessary. Then he will know it to be his real Being and thus be liberated while still living.[1]

Some armchair critics have claimed that the quest of Self-realization is arrogant or presumptuous or does not involve the humility and self-effacement of sainthood. If, instead of theorizing, they undertook the eradication of the *vasanas,* which are the roots of the ego, they would soon see. Actually it is beyond both arrogance and humility, beyond all pairs of opposites; it is simply what is. It involves not merely the humbling of the ego but its complete dissolution.

'You are the Self even now, but you confuse this present consciousness or ego with the Absolute Consciousness or Self. This false identification is due to ignorance, and ignorance disappears together with the ego. Killing the ego is the only thing to be done. Realization already exists; no attempt need be made to attain it. For it is not anything external or new to be acquired. It is always and everywhere—here and now too.'[2]

D.: This method seems to be quicker than the usual one of cultivating the virtues alleged to be necessary for Realization.

[1] T., p. 141   [2] T., p. 174

B.: Yes. All vices centre round the ego. When the ego is gone Realization results naturally.[1]

Having spoken of the saint and the mystic philosopher, mention should also be made of the occultist, that is the person who seeks Realization for the sake of the supernatural powers it may bring. This Bhagavan always discouraged. Realization may bring powers with it, as the higher includes the lower, but desire for powers will impede Realization, as the quest for the lower negates the higher. If the objective is the endowment of the ego with new powers, how can it at the same time be the liquidation of the ego? Such a person has not understood what Realization means.

D.: What are the powers of supermen?

B.: Whether the powers are high or low, whether of the mind or what you call the super-mind, they exist only with reference to him who possesses them. Find out who that is.[2]

B.: He that would abide in the Self should never swerve from his one-pointed attention to the Self or the pure Being that He is. If he slips or swerves away from that State, several kinds of vision conjured up by the mind may be seen; but one should not be misled by such visions—which may be of light or space—nor by the *nada* or subtle sounds that may be heard, nor by the visions of a personified God, seen either within oneself or outwardly, as if they had an objective reality. One should not mistake any of these things for the Reality. When the principle of intellection by which these visions etc. are cognized or perceived is itself false or illusory, how can the objects thus cognized, much less the visions perceived, be real?[3]

'There are some foolish persons who, not realizing that they themselves are moved by the Divine Power, seek to attain all supernatural powers of action. They are like the lame man who said: "I can dispose of the enemy if someone will hold me up on my legs." '

[1] T., p. 146 [2] D.D., I, p. 60 [3] S.I., p. 20

'Since peace of mind is permanent in Liberation, how can they who yoke their mind to powers—which are unattainable except through the activity of the mind—become merged in the Bliss of Liberation which subdues the agitation of the mind.'[1]

D.: Can a yogi know his past lives?

B.: Do you know the present life that you wish to know the past? Find the present, then the rest will follow. Even with your present limited knowledge, you suffer much. Why should you burden yourself with more knowledge? Is it so as to suffer more?

D.: Does Bhagavan use occult powers to make others realize the Self or is the mere fact of Bhagavan's Realization enough for that?

B.: The spiritual force of Realization is far more powerful than the use of all occult powers. Inasmuch as there is no ego in the Sage there are no 'others' for him. What is the highest benefit that can be conferred on you? It is happiness, and happiness is born of peace. Peace can reign only where there is no disturbance, and disturbance is due to thoughts that arise in the mind. When the mind is itself absent, there will be perfect peace. Unless a person has annihilated the mind, he cannot gain peace and be happy. And unless he himself is happy, he cannot bestow happiness on 'others'. Since however there are no 'others' for the Sage, who has no mind, the mere fact of his Self-realization is itself enough to make the 'others' happy too.[2]

'When asked if occult powers (*siddhis*) can be achieved with the divine state (*Isvaratva*) as mentioned in the last verse of *Dakshinamurthi Stotra,* the Maharshi said: "Let the divine state be achieved first, and then the other questions may be raised."[3]

'No powers can extend into Self-realization, so how can they extend beyond it? People who desire powers are not content with their idea of Pure Consciousness. They are inclined to neglect the supreme happiness of Realization for the sake of powers. In search of these they follow by-lanes instead of the highroad and so risk losing their way. In order to guide them aright and keep them on the highroad, they are told that powers accompany Realization. In fact Realization comprises everything and the Realized Man will not waste a thought on powers. Let people get first Realization and then seek powers if they still want to.'[1]

Powers may accrue before or after attaining Realization, or they may not, according to the nature of the person, but they are not to be valued or sought after, nor is their absence or the absence of visions or other such experiences to be taken as a cause for discouragement on the path.

D.: Is it not necessary or at least advantageous to render the body invisible in one's spiritual progress?

B.: Why do you think of that? Are you the body?

D.: No, but advanced spirituality must effect a change in the body, mustn't it?

B.: What change do you desire in the body and why?

D.: Isn't invisibility evidence of advanced wisdom (*jnana*)?

B.: In that case all those who spoke and wrote and passed their lives in the sight of others must be considered ignorant (*ajnanis*).

D.: But the sages Vasishta and Valmiki possessed such powers.

B.: It may have been their destiny (*prarabdha*) to develop such powers (*siddhis*) side by side with their widsom (*jnana*). Why should you aim at that which is not essential but is apt to prove a hindrance to wisdom (*jnana*)? Does the Sage (*jnani*) feel oppressed by his body being visible?

D.: No.

B.: A hypnotist can suddenly render himself invisible. Is he therefore a Sage?

D.: No.

[1] T., p. 57

B.: Visibility and invisibility refer to him who sees. Who is that? Solve that question first. Other questions are unimportant.[1]

An American visitor was discouraged at having attained no powers.

D.: I have been interesting myself in metaphysics for over twenty years, but I have not gained any novel experiences as so many others claim to. I have no powers of clairvoyance, clairaudience, etc. I feel locked up in this body, nothing more.

B.: That is all right. Reality is only one and that is the Self. All other things are mere phenomena in it, of it and by it. Seer, sight and seen are all the Self only. Can anyone see or hear without the Self? What difference does it make if you see or hear anyone close up or at a great distance? The organs of sight and hearing are needed in both cases. So is the mind. None of them can be dispensed with. In either case you are dependent on them. Why then should there be any clamour about clairvoyance or clairaudience? Moreover, what is acquired will also be lost in due course. It can never be permanent. The only permanent thing is Reality and that is the Self. You say: 'I am', 'I am going', 'I am speaking', 'I am working', etc. Hyphenate the 'I-am' in all of them. Thus: 'I-AM'. That is the abiding and fundamental Reality. This truth was taught by God to Moses. 'I AM that I-AM' 'Be still and know that I-AM GOD', so 'I-AM' is God.[2]

From what has been said up to here it will be seen that Self-Realization is the most simple and natural thing, in fact the only simple and natural thing, simply being what is, and yet the most rare, unknown to the saints, glimpsed briefly by the mystics. 'Among thousands there is perhaps one who strives and is perfect. Among thousands who strive and are perfect there is perhaps one who knows Me as I am.' (Bhagavad Gita, VII-3). Unfortunately it is a sign of our times that attainment of this supreme state is falsely claimed for many. The aspirant needs to discriminate.

Once attained, the Supreme State must be the same by whatever

[1] T., p. 30   [2] T., p. 503

path and whatever religion it was approached, being, by its very nature, beyond differentiation.

'Once attained, the state of Self-realization is the same by whatever path and in whatever religion it may be approached. There are three aspects of God according to one's approach to Realization. They are: *Sat* (Being), *Chit* (Consciousness), *Ananda* (Bliss).

'The aspect of Being is emphasized by *jnanis* who are said to repose in the Essence of Being after incessant search and to have their individuality lost in the Supreme.

'The Consciousness aspect is approached by yogis who exert themselves to control their breath in order to steady the mind and are then said to see the Glory (Consciousness of Being) of God as the one Light radiating in all directions.

'The Beatitude aspect is approached by devotees who become intoxicated with the nectar of love of God and lose themselves in Blissful experience. Unwilling to leave this, they remain for ever merged in God.

'The four *margas*, *Karma*, *Bhakti*, *Yoga* and *Jnana* are not exclusive of one another. They are described separately in classical works only to convey an idea of the appropriate aspect of God to appeal readily to the aspirant according to his predisposition.'[1]

Experience of Realization is known as *samadhi*. It is often supposed that *samadhi* implies trance, but that is not necessarily so. It is also possible to be in a state of *samadhi* while retaining full possession of human faculties. In fact, a Self-realized Sage such as the Maharshi is permanently in such a state. Even the preglimpses of Realization spoken of earlier do not necessarily imply trance.

'The *sannyasi* visitor, Swami Lokesananda, asked about *samadhi*.'

B.: 1. Holding on to Reality is *samadhi*.

[1] F.H., p. 70

2. Holding on to *samadhi* with effort is *savikalpa samadhi*.

3. Merging in Reality and remaining unaware of the world is *nirvikalpa samadhi*.

4. Merging in ignorance and remaining unaware of the world is sleep.

5. Remaining in the primal, pure, natural state without effort is *sahaja nirvikalpa samadhi*.'[1]

Sleep	Kevala	Sahaja
1. mind alive	1. mind alive	1. mind dead
2. sunk in oblivion	2. sunk in light	2. resolved into the Self
	3. Like a bucket with a rope left lying in the water in the well	3. Like a river discharged into the ocean and its identity lost
	4. to be drawn out by the other end of the rope	4. a river cannot be redirected from the ocean[2]

'The old gentleman asked Bhagavan whether it was not necessary to go through *nirvikalpa samadhi* first before attaining to *sahaja samadhi*. Bhagavan replied: "When we have tendencies that we are trying to give up, that is to say when we are still imperfect and have to make conscious efforts to keep the mind one-pointed or free from thought, the thoughtless state which we thus attain is *nirvikalpa samadhi*. When, through practice, we are always in that state, not going into *samadhi* and coming out again, that is the *sahaja* state. In *sahaja* one sees the only Self and sees the world as a form assumed by the Self." '[3]

The question of the nature of *samadhi* brings with it the question of activity. Uselessly trying to imagine what *samadhi* is or what

[1] T., p. 391 [2] T., p. 187 [3] D.D., II, p. 61

Realization implies, instead of striving to attain it, people form theories as to whether the Realized Man can be active or not.

D.: Can a man who has attained Realization move about and act and speak?

B.: Why not? Do you suppose Realization means being inert like a stone or becoming nothing?

D.: I don't know, but they say that the highest state is withdrawal from all sense activities, thoughts and experiences, in fact cessation of activity.

B.: Then how would it differ from deep sleep? Besides, it would be a state which, however exalted, comes and goes and would therefore not be the natural and normal state, so how could it represent the eternal presence of the Supreme Self, which persists through all states, and survives them? It is true that there is such a state and that in the case of some people it may be necessary to go through it. It may be a temporary phase of the quest or persist to the end of a man's life, if it be the Divine Will or the man's destiny, but in any case you cannot call it the highest state. If it were you would have to say that not only the Sages, but God Himself has not attained the highest state, since not only are the Realized Sages very active but the Personal God (Isvara) himself is obviously not in this supremely inactive state, since He presides over the world and directs its activities.[1]

D.: What is *samadhi*?

B.: In yoga the term is used to indicate some kind of trance and there are various kinds of *samadhi*. But the *samadhi* I speak to you about is different. It is *sahaja samadhi*. In this state you remain calm and composed during activity. You realize that you are moved by the deeper Real Self within and are unaffected by what you do or say or think. You have no worries, anxieties or cares, for you realize that there is nothing that belongs to you as ego and that everything is being done by something with which you are in conscious union.[2]

[1] S.D.B., ix   [2] S.D.B., xi

After Realization a man may continue a life of worldly activity or not; it makes no difference to his state.

'A visitor said: Realized men generally withdraw from active life and abstain from worldly activity.'

B.: They may or may not. Some even after Realization carry on trade or business or rule a kingdom. Some withdraw to solitary places and abstain from all activity more than the minimum necessary to keep life in the body. We cannot make any general rule about it.[1]

Inability to understand the apparent inactivity of the Sage is one of the difficulties of many Western writers. Firmly convinced that Christ was mistaken in saying that Mary had chosen the better part, modern Christians are apt to represent Martha, the outwardly active one, as superior and to criticize the Sage for what they consider inaction.

When asked by an aspirant whether his Realization, if attained, would help others, Bhagavan has been known to reply:

'Yes, and it is the best help you possibly can give them.'

But then he added:

'But in fact there are no others to help.'

The same paradox is proclaimed in Buddhism where, for instance in the Diamond Sutra, after speaking of compassion, the Buddha explains that in reality there are no others to be compassionate to. The Lord Buddha continued: Do not think, Subhuti, that the Tathagata would consider within himself: I will deliver human beings. That would be degrading thought. Why? Because there are really no sentient beings to be delivered by the Tathagata. Should there be any sentient beings to be delivered by the Tathagata, it would mean that the Tathagata was cherishing within his mind arbitrary conceptions of phenomena such as one's own self, other selves, living beings and an

[1] D.D., II, p. 95

universal self. Even when the Tathagata refers to himself, he is not holding within his mind any such arbitrary thought. Only terrestrial human beings think of selfhood as being a personal possession. Subhuti, even the expression 'terrestrial beings' as used by the Tathagata does not mean that there are any such beings. It is only used as a figure of speech.[1]

'People often say that a Realized Man should go about preaching his message. They ask how a man can remain quiet in Realization when there is misery also existing. But what is a Realized Man? Does he see misery outside himself? They want to determine his state without themselves realizing it. From his standpoint their contention amounts to this: a man has a dream in which he sees a number of persons. On waking up he asks, "Have the people in the dream also woke up?" It is ridiculous. Again, some good man says, "It does not matter even if I don't get Realization. Or let me be the last man in the world to get it so that I can help all others to become Realized before I do." That is just like the dreamer saying: "Let all these people in the dream wake up before I do." He would be no more absurd than this amiable philosopher.'[2]

And yet, paradoxically, the Sage is intensely active, although he may apparently be inactive.

'A saying of Laotse from the Tao Te King was read out in the hall: "By his non-action, the Sage governs all." Sri Bhagavan remarked: "Non-action is unceasing activity. The Sage is characterized by eternal and incessant activity. His stillness is like the apparent stillness of a fast rotating top. It is moving too fast for the eye to see, so it appears to be still. Yet it is rotating. So is the apparent inaction of the Sage. This has to be explained because people generally mistake his stillness for inertness. It is not so." '[3]

Similar to this preoccupation with action was the question whether

---

[1] From *A Buddhist Bible*, by Dwight Goddard, quoted in *Buddhism and Christianity in the light of Hinduism*, by Arthur Osborne, p. 114.
[2] T., p. 498   [3] T., p. 599

the Realized Man is bound by destiny. Really the question has no meaning. His body is bound by destiny, but, since he does not identify himself with the body, its destiny cannot bind him. Being one with the Eternal Self within which this body, this life, this world, passes like an appearance, he cannot be bound by anything.

'This morning a visitor said to Bhagavan: "The Realized Man has no *karma*; he is not bound by destiny, so why should he still retain a body?"'

B.: Who asks this question—a Realized Man or an unrealized? Why worry about what the Realized Man does or why he does anything? Better think about yourself.

'He was then silent. After a while, however, he explained further, "You are under the impression that you are the body, so you think the Realized Man has also a body. Does he say that he has? He may seem to you to have one and do things with it, as others do. The charred ashes of a rope look like a rope but are no use to tie anything with. So long as one identifies oneself with the body, all this is hard to understand. That is why it is sometimes said in answer to such questions that the body of the Realized Man continues to exist until his destiny has worked itself out and then falls away. An example of this that is sometimes given is that an arrow which has been loosed from the bow (destiny) must continue it course and hit the mark even though the animal that stood there has moved away and another has taken its place (Realization has been achieved). But the truth is that the Realized Man has transcended all destiny and is bound neither by the body nor by its destiny.'[1]

Equally beside the point is the question whether the Realized Man can feel pain or pleasure (if pleasure, then pain also, because the two go together; they are a pair of opposites).

'The sensation is common both to the Realized Man and the

[1] D. D., II, p. 301

unrealized. The difference is that the unrealized man identifies himself with the body that feels it, whereas the Realized Man knows that all this is Self, all this is Brahman. If there is pain let it be; it is also part of the Self and the Self is perfect.'[1]

Or whether he can commit sin. The very raising of this question implies failure to understand what is meant by Self-Realization. Sin is the action of the ego or the individual being in its own interests against the universal harmony or the Will of God. But where there is no ego, where there is only the Universal Self, who is to act against whom?

'An unrealized man sees one who is Realized and identifies him with the body. Because he does not know the Self and mistakes the body for the Self, he extends the same mistake to the body of the Realized Man. The latter is therefore considered to be the physical form. Again, the unrealized man, though in fact not the originator of his actions, imagines himself to be so, and considers the actions of the body as his own and therefore thinks the Realized Man to be so acting when the body is active. But the latter knows the truth and is not deceived. His state cannot be understood by the unrealized and therefore the question of his actions troubles the latter although it does not arise for him himself.[2]

'All good or divine qualities are included in *Jnana* (spiritual Enlightenment) and all bad or satanic qualities in *ajnana* (spiritual darkness). When *jnana* comes all *ajnana* goes, so that all divine qualities come automatically. If a man is a *Jnani* he cannot utter lies or commit any sin.'[3]

The saying that there is no ego or that the mind is dead sometimes leads to misunderstandings. What is meant is simply that the mind or ego as apparent creator or originator of policies, plans and ideas is dead. Understanding remains, and pure radiant Consciousness.

[1] T., p. 383   [2] T., p. 499   [3] D.D., I, p. 69

D.: Can we think without the mind?

B.: Thoughts can continue like other activities. They do not disturb the Supreme Consciousness.[1]

B.: People surmise the existence of the pure mind in the *jivanmukta* and the personal God. They ask how he could otherwise live and act. But this is only a concession to argument. The pure mind is in fact the Absolute Consciousness. The object to be witnessed and the witness finally merge together and Absolute Consciousness alone remains. It is not a state of blank or ignorance but is the Supreme Self.[2]

The mind of the Realized Man is sometimes compared to the moon in daytime.

'The moon shines by reflecting the light of the sun. When the sun has set, the moon is useful for displaying objects. When the sun has risen no one needs the moon, though its disc is visible in the sky. So it is with the mind and the Heart. The mind is made useful by its reflected light. It is used for seeing objects. When turned inwards it merges into the source of illumination which shines by itself and the mind is then like the moon in daytime.'[3]

Sometimes people expressed fear at the thought of giving up the ego, but Bhagavan reminded them that they do so every time they go to sleep.

'People are afraid that when the ego or the mind is killed, the result may be a mere blank and not happiness. What really happens is that the thinker, the object of thought and thinking all merge in the one Source which is Consciousness and Bliss itself, and thus that state is neither inert nor blank. I don't understand why people should be afraid of a state in which all thoughts cease to exist and the mind is killed. They daily experience it in

[1] T., p. 43   [2] T., p. 68   [3] M.G., I, p. 17

sleep. There is no mind or thought in sleep. Yet when one rises from sleep one says, "I slept well".[1]

Moreover, in sleep they surrender the ego in order to lapse into a mere blank, whereas Realization is merging into pure Consciousness which is the uttermost Bliss.

'In answer to a visitor Bhagavan made the following remark: You can have, or rather you will yourself be, the highest imaginable kind of happiness. All other kinds of happiness which you have spoken of as "pleasure", "joy", "happiness", "bliss", are only reflections of the *Ananda* which, in your true nature, you are.'[2]

It is impossible to describe *samadhi* since it transcends the mind. It can only be experienced.

'An American lady asked Bhagavan what his experiences of *samadhi* were. When it was suggested that she should relate her experiences and ask if they were right, she replied that Sri Bhagavan's experiences ought to be correct and should be known whereas her own were unimportant. She wanted to know if Sri Bhagavan felt his body hot or cold in *samadhi,* if he spent the first three years and a half of his stay in Tiruvannamalai in prayer and so on.'

B.: Samadhi transcends mind and speech and cannot be described. Even the state of deep sleep cannot be described; the state of *samadhi* even less.

D.: But I know that I was unconscious in deep sleep.

B.: Consciousness and unconsciousness are modes of the mind. *Samadhi* transcends the mind.

D.: Still, you can say what it is like.

B.: You will know only when you are in *samadhi*.[3]

Sometimes he referred to the cinema screen as an illustration.

[1] D.D., II, p. 83   [2] D.D., I, p. 15   [3] T., p. 110

D.: If the Realized and the unrealized alike perceive the world, where is the difference between them?

B.: When the Realized Man sees the world he sees the Self that is the substratum of all that is seen. Whether the unrealized man sees the world or not, he is ignorant of his true being, the Self. Take the example of a film on a cinema screen. What is there in front of you before the film begins? Only the screen. On that screen you see the entire show, and to all appearances the pictures are real. But go and try to take hold of them and what do you take hold of? The screen on which the pictures appear so real. After the play, when the pictures disappear, what remains? The screen again. So it is with the Self. That alone exists; the pictures come and go. If you hold on to the Self, you will not be deceived by the appearance of the pictures. Nor does it matter at all whether the pictures appear or disappear.[1]

Once permanent, unwavering *sahaja samadhi* has been obtained, this is the state of *Mukti* or Liberation. People speak of *jivanmukti* and *videhamukti*, that is Liberation while still living and Liberation after death, but Bhagavan explained that the difference is only from the point of view of the observer; to the Realized Man himself it makes no difference whether he wears a body or not.

'Mr. Bannerjee asked Bhagavan what is the difference between *jivanmukti and videhamukti.*'

B.: There is no difference. For those who ask it is said that a Realized Man with a body is a *jivanmukta* and that he attains *videhamukti* when he sheds the body, but this difference exists only for the onlooker, not for him. His state is the same before shedding the body and after. We think of him as a human form or as being in that form, but he knows that he is the Self, the One Reality, both inner and outer, which is not bound by any form. There is a verse in the Bhagavatha (Bhagavan here quoted the verse in Tamil) which says that just as a drunken man does not notice whether he is wearing his shawl or whether it has fallen

[1] M.G., p. 58

off, so the Realized Man is hardly aware of his body and it makes no difference to him whether it remains or drops off.[1]

'There are no stages in Realization or *Mukti*. There are no degrees of Liberation. So there cannot be one stage of Liberation with the body and another when the body has been shed. The Realized Man knows that he is the Self and that nothing, neither his body nor anything else, exists but for the Self. To such a one what difference could the presence or absence of a body make?'[2]

Sometimes Realization is called *Turiya*, the 'Fourth State', because it underlies the three states of waking, dream and deep sleep.

'When I entered the hall Bhagavan was answering some questions and was saying: "There is no difference between the dream and waking states except that the former is short and the latter long. Both are the product of the mind. Because the waking state lasts longer we imagine it to be our real state; but actually our real state is what is sometimes called the Fourth State, which is always as it is, and is unaffected by waking, dream or sleep. Because we call these three "states" we call that a state also; however, it is really just the natural state of the Self. A "fourth" state would imply something relative, whereas this is transcendent." '[3]

In truth, there is no bondage.

'Our real nature is Liberation, but we imagine that we are bound and make strenuous efforts to get free, although all the while we are free. This is understood only when we reach that state. Then we shall be surprised to find that we were frantically striving to attain something that we always were and are. An illustration will make this clear. A man goes to sleep in this hall. He dreams he has gone on a world-tour and is travelling over hill and dale, forest and plain, desert and sea, across various

[1] D.D., II, p. 109   [2] D.D., II, p. 110   [3] D.D., II, p. 100

continents, and after many years of weary and strenuous travel, returns to this country, reaches Tiruvannamalai, enters the Asramam and walks into the hall. Just at that moment he wakes up and finds that he has not moved at all but has been sleeping where he lay down. He has not returned after great efforts to this hall, but was here all the time. It is exactly like that. If it is asked why, being free, we imagine ourselves bound, I answer, "Why, being in the hall, did you imagine you were on a world-tour, crossing hill and dale, desert and sea?" It is all in the mind or *maya*.'[1]

'8. Under whatever name and form one may worship the Absolute Reality, it is only a means for Realizing It without name and form. That alone is true Realization, wherein one knows oneself in relation to that Reality, attains peace and realizes one's identity with it.

'9. The duality of subject and object, the trinity of seer, sight and seen, can exist only if supported by the One. If one turns inwards in search of that One Reality they fall away. Those who see this are those who see Wisdom. They are never in doubt.

'21. What is the truth of the scriptures which declare that if one sees the Self one sees God? How can one see one's Self? If, since one is a single being, one cannot see one's Self, how can one see God? Only by becoming a prey to Him.

'22. The Divine gives light to the mind and shines within it. Except by turning the mind inwards and fixing it in the Divine, there is no other way to know Him through the mind.

'30. If one enquires "Who am I?" within the mind, the individual "I" falls down abashed as soon as one reaches the Heart and immediately Reality manifests itself spontaneously as "I-I". Although it reveals itself as the "I" it is not the ego but the Perfect Being, the Absolute Self.

'31. For him who is immersed in the Bliss of the Self, arising from the extinction of the ego, what remains to be accomplished?

[1] D.D., II, p. 101

He is not aware of anything other than the Self. Who can comprehend his state?

'32. Although the scriptures proclaim "Thou art That" it is only a sign of weakness of mind to meditate, "I am That, not this", because you are eternally That. What has to be done is to investigate what one really is and remain That.

'33. It is ridiculous to say either "I have not realized the Self" or "I have realized the Self"; are there two selves for one to be the object of the other's realization? It is a truth within the experience of everyone that there is only one Self.

'34. It is due to illusion born of ignorance that men fail to recognize That which is always and for everybody the inherent Reality dwelling in its natural Heart-centre and to abide in it, and that instead they argue that it exists or does not exist, that it has form or has not form, or is non-dual or dual.

'35. To seek and abide in the Reality that is always attained is the only Attainment. All other attainments (*siddhis*) are such as are acquired in dreams. Can they that are established in the Reality and are free from *maya* be deluded by them?

'38. As long as a man is the doer, he also reaps the fruits of his deeds, but as soon as he realizes the Self through enquiry as to who is the doer, his sense of being the doer falls away and the triple *karma* is ended. This is the state of eternal Liberation.

'39. Only so long as one considers oneself bound do thoughts of bondage and Liberation continue. When one enquires who is bound the Self is realized, eternally attained, eternally free. When thought of bondage comes to an end, can thought of Liberation survive?

'40. If it is said that Liberation is of three kinds, with form, or without form, or with and without form, then let me tell you that the extinction of the three forms of Liberation is the only true Liberation.'

(*F. V.*)

INDEX